beloved
on the earth

beloved
on the earth:

150 POEMS
OF GRIEF
AND
GRATITUDE

Edited by Jim Perlman, Deborah Cooper,
Mara Hart and Pamela Mittlefehldt

HOLY COW! PRESS :: DULUTH, MINNESOTA :: 2009

Permissions and additional copyright notices appear on pages 246-251; copyrights for the individual poems in this collection are held by their authors.

Cover artwork: screen print by Joel Cooper. Cover and text design by Clarity (Duluth, Minnesota). Printed in Canada. First printing, 2009.

Co-editors photograph, copyright ©2009 by Julia Cheng.

10 9 8 7 6 5 4 3 2

This project is supported in part by grant awards from the Paula and Cy DeCosse Fund of The Minneapolis Foundation, The Lenfestey Family Foundation, The Elmer L. & Eleanor J. Andersen Foundation, Overman Charitable Trust, and by gifts from generous donors.

Holy Cow! Press books are distributed to the trade by Consortium Book Sales & Distribution, c/o Perseus Distribution, 1094 Flex Drive, Jackson, Tennessee 38301.

For personal inquiries, write to:
Holy Cow! Press,
Post Office Box 3170, Mount Royal Station,
Duluth, Minnesota 55803.

Please visit our website: www.holycowpress.org

Library of Congress Cataloging-in-Publication Data

Beloved on the Earth : 150 poems of grief and gratitude / edited by Jim Perlman ... [et al.].
p. cm.
ISBN 978-0-9779458-9-4 (alk. paper)
1. Death—Poetry. 2. Grief—Poetry. 3. Loss (Psychology)—Poetry. 4. Bereavement—Poetry. I. Perlman, Jim, 1951-
PN6110.D4B35 2009
808.81'9354—dc22   2009009163

We dedicate this poetry anthology
in blessed memory of our beloved ones:

*For Jim Perlman's parents, Grace Audrey Feinberg Perlman
and Everett C. Perlman*

---

*For Deborah Cooper's parents, Jack and Colleen Gordon
and for her brother, Drew Gordon*

---

*For Mara Hart's husband, Robert Hart (1920-2008)
and for her parents, Lucile Dvorak and George Kirk*

---

*For Pamela Mittlefehldt's parents, Leatha Muriel Ferguson
Klass and Walter Kottler Klass*

TABLE OF CONTENTS

DEAR READER: A PREFACE

WE TURN TO POEMS FOR SOLACE, WISDOM, COMFORT, JOY. We wrap ourselves in words—words of mourning and grief, words of mystery, words of gratitude and remembrance. As unique as each life is, so is each death. And yet, in our isolated grief and mourning, we turn to the comfort, the embrace of the words of others.

Poetry crystallizes emotion and language. The concise clarity of a poem creates a unique space within which to mourn while knowing we are not alone. This collection of poems on grief and gratitude honors the individual lives of those departed, our beloved on this earth. It also raises a collective song of shared loss and sorrow.

Four friends, each mourning the loss of loved ones, each comforting the others in the time of their own loss. Jim Perlman, editor and publisher of Holy Cow! Press had mentioned that he was planning to create an anthology of poems on grief and gratitude after his mother passed away in late February, 2007. His frustration was that poems of mourning, consolation and insight were found scattered in many places—in prayer books, individual poets' collections and elsewhere. Mara, Deborah and Pamela began talking with him about the project. As the discussions unfolded, we became co-editors, and also fellow travelers on this journey through the country of grief and gratitude.

A public call for poems was issued in national, regional and local writers' newsletters and magazines. We were astounded by the response; over two thousand poems were received. For months, we immersed ourselves in the heartbreak, bittersweet memories, and love of hundreds of poets. Some were established voices, known to us, but many of the poems were from poets who were new to us. Sorting through this incredible response was a gift. It was also one of the most difficult aspects of this project.

The hundreds of submitted poems were an amazing expression of love, pain, loss, wonder, celebration, healing. It was an honor to read each of them. As we approached the process of selecting which poems would be appropriate for this volume, we agreed on several criteria. The poems needed to have a universality, even as each poem honored an individual. Poems that specifically detailed the life of an individual were oftentimes moving, but almost too intimate for a more general readership. We wanted poems that we could enter easily and then feel as if the poems spoke about a larger, shared experience. We looked for unique images, memorable ways of expressing loss and grief. Loss is such a universal emotion, and yet our ways of describing it often seem limited. Death is never a cliché, and yet our language for describing it tends to be repetitive. We considered craft, length, and honesty of emotion. Perhaps ultimately it came down to which poems moved us— which poems spoke most intensely and directly to our hearts.

Initially, we had thought of organizing the book by topic: death of parents, siblings, a beloved friend, extended family. However, it soon became clear that we couldn't always identify for whom the poem was written, and many poems fit into a number of categories. We settled eventually on organizing the volume alphabetically by author—primarily because there is no innate order or hierarchy in this collection. The poems build upon each other, embrace each other, grow from each other.

There is an index at the end of the book. We asked the poets to identify indexing categories. But again, there was so much overlapping that we decided to identify those poems that clearly were about a specific topic. If one is seeking a poem about the death of a mother, the index will provide an initial guide, but so many other poems may be equally appropriate.

Our hope is that these poems, these finely honed words and images, will enlarge our capacity to grieve, will open us to the healing and grace that come from mourning, honoring, and celebrating our beloved on this earth.

—*Pamela Mittlefehldt*, March, 2009

LATE FRAGMENT

Raymond Carver

And did you get what
you wanted from this life, even so?
I did.
And what did you want?
To call myself beloved, to feel myself
beloved on the earth.

SPIRIT BUNDLE FOR DIANE

Marian Aitches

"*Lakota people honor loved ones who have died
by preparing a bundle. They stay with the spirit
until they are ready to let it go.*" —Ella Cara Deloria

Sister,
I will keep you with me a while.
I have smoothed your magenta scarf, spread
the silk

      with a lock of chestnut hair folded in a leaf
      of paper you sent long ago.
      You wrote just one word. *Mim.*
      —signed with only the letter *D*;
      the white space before
      my eyes bloomed
      like a desert flower after
      rain, a rich and silent language.

      Here is the turquoise elephant I brought
      you from Chiang Mai—
      and your lapis stones, diamonds for those
      who love color more than light.
      The book of poems you marked
      with a blue jay feather, writing in the margins,
      Look at the man who sings to animals
      who sleeps smiling in the jungle
      while we, in narrow beds, dream
      of falling off cliffs and wake afraid.

I will bring you yellow roses, white irises
and cashew chicken—fried shrimp, garlic spinach,
things you loved but could not relish
at the end of this world. We will drink red wine
together and remember leaning back to back
against each other—laughing, dreaming of being
beautiful old ladies charming gray-haired men.

BURIAL AT SEA

Diane Averill

On the ferry between Seattle
and Port Angeles, each of my sisters
holds a handful of Mother-ashes.
I hide in a seagull's eyes.
As they let her go,
grit and bits of bone,
I hear a voice
calling from a cell phone
in the ashy palm of
a sister's hand.
As I light gray and white
on the railing,
the sea becomes sun's summer
morning. My sister says into the phone
*Mom is sitting here with us
in the form of a gull.*
On the railing
the sea turns rose in the gull's eyes,
and that's how I know this voice of mine
isn't really me at all—
my lips full of ashes
disappearing into water.

A Lesson in Plate Tectonics
October 22, 2006

Cynthia M. Baer

The plates shift, soundless, underground
the world is forever altered. Not so

the heavens. Up on Highlands sky opens
onto cloudscapes that have drifted

overnight. Thin veneer of yesterday's
masses, scattered to patches that catch

the light and bask in its brilliance,
only to cast it aside, slip into shadow.

Nothing permanent, says the sky. The land lies.
Trees stand today where yesterday they stood.

The canyon spreads, hills rolling but unmoved.
The spall at my feet lies still at my feet.

Invisible, the slow moving movements
of the land. Not like sky-scudding clouds

whose face changes with every breath of wind
and with the infinite play of light.

No, earth moves in increments unremarkable
monumental. Unseen, unheard, plates shift

ground gives; life rides the swells of a world
forever altered. For instance, you're gone.

THE ROLE OF ELEGY

Mary Jo Bang

The role of elegy is
To put a mask on tragedy,
A drape on the mirror.
To bow to the cultural

Debate over the aesthetization of sorrow,
Of loss, of the unbearable
Afterimage of the once material,
To look for an imagined

Consolidation of grief
So we can all be finished
Once and for all and genuinely shut up
The cabinet of genuine particulars.

Instead there's the endless refrain
One hears replayed repeatedly
Through the just ajar door:
Some terrible mistake has been made.

What is elegy but the attempt
To rebreathe life
Into what the gone one once was
Before he grew to enormity.

Come on stage and be yourself,
The elegist says to the dead. Show them
Now—after the fact—
What you were meant to be:

The performer of a live song.
A shoe. Now bow.
What is left but this:
The compulsion to tell.

The transient distraction of ink on cloth
One scrubbed and scrubbed
But couldn't make less
Not then, not soon.

Each day, a new caption on the cartoon
Ending that simply cannot be.
One hears repeatedly, the role of elegy is.

GHAZAL FOR MY MOTHER

Jackie Bartley

Henna freckles blossomed on the flat plains of my mother's hands.
Red-knuckled hills and rugged cuticles mapped my mother's hands.

She filled a steno pad beside our phone with shorthand notes,
a penciled trail of slashes and swirls in my mother's hand.

At bedtime, princesses danced and dreamed, witches cast their spells.
Fairy tales and far-off lands opened in my mother's hands.

Suits took shape from finest wools, skirts from brushed linen;
prom gowns grew from remnants of silk brocade in my mother's hands.

She sealed peach pies and fluted their crusts like fine-wrought silver.
Skittish butterflies across the kitchen table, my mother's hands.

When sleep came hard or dreams alarmed, she drew up the covers.
Across my cheek when my words came sharp, my mother's hand.

She taught me night, the stars, the names of northern constellations.
In pale, rigid skies, a dozen moons rose in my mother's hands.

What are they now in the land of the dead, my mother's hands?
Across the page, I write these words in my mother's hand.

ENDING WITH A LINE FROM LEAR

Marvin Bell

I will try to remember. It was light.
It was also dark, in the grave. I could feel
how dark it was, how black it would be
without my father. When he was gone.
But he was not gone, not yet. He was only
a corpse, and I could still touch him
that afternoon. Earlier the same afternoon.
This is the one thing that scares me:
losing my father. I don't want him to go.
I am a young man. I will never be older.
I am wearing a tie and a watch. The sky,
gray, hangs over everything. Today
the sky has no curve to it, and no end.
He is deep into his mission. He has business
to attend to. He wears a tie but no watch.
I will skip a lot of what happens next.
Then the moment comes. Everything, everything
has been said, and the wheels start to turn.
They roll, the straps unwind, and the coffin
begins to descend. Into the awful damp.
Into the black center of the earth. I
am being left behind. The center of my body
sinks down into the cold fire of the grave.
But still my feet stand on top of the dirt.
My father's grave. I will never again.
Never. Never. Never. Never. Never.

Ritual #3

Cal Benson

Long ago the full September moon brought
you to us, and just last June another
rising moon carefully took you away.

With each returning moon you revisit —
though only in the night — reminding me
more of your death than your birth, but bringing

joy; then the waning moon takes you away
again. In every season, I watch for
the long shadows that lounge across the snow

or grass or autumn leaves. As I talk to
moons' round faces, I talk to you, welcome
your arrival and tell you never to

worry that you two are going away,
because in thirty nights you will return.

The Wish to Be Generous

Wendell Berry

All that I serve will die, all my delights,
the flesh kindled from my flesh, garden and field,
the silent lilies standing in the woods,
the woods, the hill, the whole earth, all
will burn in man's evil, or dwindle
in its own age. Let the world bring on me
the sleep of darkness without stars, so I may know
my little light taken from me into the seed
of the beginning and the end, so I may bow
to mystery, and take my stand on the earth
like a tree in a field, passing without haste
or regret toward what will be, my life
a patient willing descent into the grass.

FACT IS

Barbara Blatner

I stare
out your kitchen window
at green-black
mountain swelling
above back yard
fields and orchards.

near the summit
before the stony
escarpment
near the vertical scar
cut through trees
for telephone wire,
a hawk
is flying.

and I'm thinking:
it doesn't matter
that you neglected us
got drunk at us
charmed us
divided us
in war
against each other.
we love you terribly,
the eye of love's
even sharper
now that you lie
in bed in your room

at the end of the hall
dying.

we're bound to you
like that hawk
to her hunger,
we hunt
your love
we circle
we shadow

CRUELTIES OF THE SUN

Barbara Blatner

lying in bed
this morning
two hundred miles
from your
house and lawn,
looking out the window, I can't see
the source of light
its bulb is burred
in fields of
cloud, but the power
of that sun is on,
gotta be, first week
of April, lemony
April, month
of your birth day.

so the legion
daffodils must be
shining down the margins
of your lawn
and all over the grass
by the entrance
to your road,
two and three clumped
everywhere,
ready for the vase
and the bee.

the guy who built your house
30 yrs ago planted
over twelve varieties
of the canary
flower. who'd imagine
there were so many
kinds to mime
the trumpet
sun, to call it forth, so many
to come back
so soon so bright
from soil's
packed coffins.

this gauzed
sun will
bruise me into
days without you,
world without
end. but year
after year
your daffodils
will sound up
easy, swift
flotillas,
come as you are,
spinning in
and out of light

FROM THIS DISTANCE

Gary Boelhower

The slight shudder as the plane lifts,
surrenders its earthly obligations.
Details blur into patterns of patchwork.
Highways and rivers, cursive loops
and lines on the diary of acres, miles, lifetimes.
From this distance I can forgive you
again. Boy Scout award dinners without you,
the only words of love slurred after a litany
of beers softens your raw edges, the fear
of another fight with mom, threatening
fists, curses, thrown things. This grief
has been a slow letting go of the small
failures of your fatherhood. From this high
window, I have a larger view, your own
father's insults and judgments, the low
wages, unpaid bills, power turned off,
your dead sister never mentioned.
Not excuses, just a way of seeing.
This grief is a long loneliness of not
feeling the touch you so wanted to give.

LOST IN THE WOODS: A BLESSING

Kathleen Sheeder Bonanno

When you are certainly lost,
when the wind blows acutely,
when the moon is unavailable,
when tragedy catches up
and walks,
like a companion, by your side,
when the snowflakes fall
severely;
then,

may you see a window and a pallid light,
may the light get bolder
as you get closer,
may the light be the sound
of vital laughing,
may the laugh be the laugh
of the ones you're missing,
may your feet find their way
to the oaken door,
may the door swing open, sure
and slow,
may each kind glad face
turn
to yours.

URGENCY

Annie Breitenbucher

Tonight the breeze is just so.
It stirs your ashes
in the bowl of my heart, just
so I know you are there. You,

all of you who are love
returned to dust.

All day it has been this way.
The sun shining just so.
This restless stirring
to know I am here. Me,

all of me, becoming love
before dust.

POEM FOR MY MOTHER

Nancy Brewka-Clark

Not having her in the world
is the strangest thing. Right now,
a winter wind is blowing sunlight
against the treetops, smashing it
into a million atoms of joy.

She herself found joy in every
lucent leaf, each kiss of transient
breeze against the cheek of
the earth. She watched the short,
sweet month of February with its
red hearts, lace and lengthening
light, the promissory note
of spring, come due with
interest every year, never jaded,
always mailing a card with
Xs and Os to her middle-aged
daughters. When she died we said
it was time, at eighty-eight, no
broken hearts here, she had a full
life, she was ailing, she was failing.

But in this light, with the snow
dripping off the roof and the branches
tossing, this light like a voice calling to
the sleeping bulbs, the burrowing
roots, this breath of fresh wind with
its sting and its kiss, as much as I
honor the spirit, I ache to touch flesh.

THE DAY BEFORE YOU DIED...

Emily K. Bright

nothing remarkable happened. Dawn
hummed with lobster boats.
Your flowers bloomed red and gold,
the same as yesterday.
Someone thought to see about lunch
and everyone took naps as usual, books
on sleeping chests rising and
sinking with the tide.

We watched the sea.
Our recent neighbors' wharf juts,
unweathered pine, across our window view,
stretching out beyond the rocks to where
low tide won't beach the dock.
We used to search for heather there,
in low August tide.
Purple bunches dried in every doorway.
You, shrunken even in my memory,
never had to bend to pass from room to room.

Everything but that new dock is weathered now
and sleeping, having soaked up enough salt
to last another lifetime.
The doctors could find nothing wrong, no reason
oxygen refused to spread to all your organs,
except that all your organs weathered
eighty-something years, the sea,
three children, traveling to India.

You saw docks come to blend in with the coast,
saw the children raise their children.

That evening, we still believed the changes
washing toward Maine would yet
be swept away to sea. We waited
for the sudden surge of wind.
But that night, the waves moved gently,
and the fog prepared itself for morning.

SKY TRAIL

Joseph Bruchac

in memory of my grandparents Jesse and Marion Bowman

I cannot count
how many times
I cried after they died.

Season after season
I was rain on salt,
salt melted by incessant rain;
a blind stone dropped
into a black sea
and sinking, sinking,
deeper, deeper.

The dream that rode me as a child
came to replace my waking life—
the world split asunder
by a great explosion,
my part spinning off
to the darkness of space
as I woke to a
bitter and bloodless half moon
hopeless and stark in morning sky.

Then, one night I looked up
remembered the stars,
saw those birds of heaven
forming a trail.

And the Night Traveler's face
became once again
a calm grandmother's gaze
guiding me toward dawn.

Now when others
speak their sorrow
I know where
to point a hand.

TO ERNESTO TREJO IN THE OTHER WORLD

Christopher Buckley

Still tonight, the stars are where we left them,
Nonchalant, incontestable in their distance.

Once we were those stars—all of us atoms
No memory will admit. And once it mattered

What we made of stars, and read into the sky;
But this evening words scatter like blackbirds

From a field, there, against the unrequited blue.
I have no idea, truly, where you are—dry wind

In eucalyptus, sedan of clouds pearl-edged in the west.
The soul could well be that cloud in the empty shape

Of clouds given the spare charities of Time, available
To us all. I wonder if you see the winos who never left

The Eagle Café, the solar systems of grease spinning
On their late nite specials, if you see all the way

To Spain, a country you never knew? Speculation is
You can see it all—down *Diagonal* or out 46, stone-blazing

Afternoons in Madera or *Madrid*, or in Barcelona
The evening walking bejeweled into the bay.

In Fresno, I remember only one guitar that spoke
Of the sea, and a cypress or two along Van Ness,

And no sea of course, no Ramblas with caged birds
Reciting in their paradisiacal tongues, no dusty angels

High in the sycamores who, if they could, would descend
For a drink at one of the chrome tables in the shade.

So many gone now, who knows if you could meet up
With anyone on Olive Street and praise the great poets

Of Spain that the good middle class assassinated in their sleep.
We never talked of the Alhambra or the Alcazar, intricate

Tile work and end rhymes imported by the colonial Moors—
Only of the *cante jondo* in the south, the bleached

Refrain of waves along the beach at Castelldefels,
And as often as not, the lost continents of the moon.

Whatever is out there is here, just as well. And so
I remind you of Rome where Giordano Bruno proclaimed

A plurality of worlds, a belief I almost maintain,
Excepting the examinations by iron and fire.

So crows today are just crows, happy to hop about
Suburban lawns without an inner life. This is the world

And it happens to us here, nothing else stands for the sky,
Weak and frayed as it is with our conjecture. Nevertheless,

I accede to a lyric mantilla of stars, a mythopoeic light
Filtering down far stanzas of the dark as evidence,

Perhaps, of hope. There is no other light, and we have
Gone through eons worth of it with less and less to show.

Is there any way, my friend, to tell us where we are
Headed tonight? I cannot see beyond Miramar Point,

That small shore of childhood where I was content
With the omnipresent salt air, the mocking bird's

Subterfuge in the pines, where I stand, feet in the cold
Sand, a tide rising, the sea reflecting the clear light

Of space back into space—the anaphora of the heart
Holding on before God, or light, or none of the above.

POEM IN OCTOBER

Andrea Hollander Budy

after Dylan Thomas

It was my twenty-third year and heaven
broke away from my reach as I stood

at her grave. Rain carved
the morning's stone face into the earth,

and the sky grayed and lowered
until they were one. Back by the trees

men smoked, as if they had nothing
better to do. But I knew as soon as I left

they would cover even
the roses my father, brother and I

had tossed upon her as if our wishing
could do what prayer had not.

When I finally left, I thought her
gone. I am fifty-four. I was wrong.

MAPLE TREES AND UNEXPECTED SNOW

Cullen Bailey Burns

Winter comes, sometimes,
when we're not done with fall—

all this snow on the crimson leaves,
the mother sitting down in her chair

to die. This is not winter
proper but serves the purpose

of forbearance. And when we are empty,
the anchors of our bones

weigh us to the snow, the trees,
the silver light

obliterating the familiar horizon.

CRADLE

Sharon M. Carter

for J.F.C. 1921-1999

It is not easy
to sleep in the bed in which you died.
I cradle my body
in the mattress hollow—
your soft sarcophagus.

In this bed you fought
for every molecule of air,
ribs and diaphragm straining
against a tumorous river.

Sleep is a galaxy away.
I lay my head
on your feather pillow
and listen
to the night breathe slowly.

On My Mother's Death: Harvesting

Sharon Chmielarz

In this north where combines cut swaths
through the wheat's blond wall, she stares
out the station window, looking for clouds
of dark smoke and the train wheels' rumbling.

She will not be afraid to start anew,
to leave the station the field dwarfs,
or the gray-roofed house, the one
where she lived. The one where we live.

When the iron horse shakes the platform,
she'll board, saying, "What a lovely
thing to find." And I'll wave goodbye.
What a lovely thing to lose.

REINS

Sharon Chmielarz

In the kitchen,
that small space
between porch door and oven,
my mother stood behind me
and braided my hair,
a sun-bleached mane in her hands.

Three strands she wove
over and under, a design
twisting the future
with the lost, her past,
until two long ropes
hung down my back.

On this dreamy morning,
long after her funeral,
my mother tugs, left
and right on my head,
in no hurry, she nor I,
to let go.

FATHER'S DIAGNOSIS: NAMING NAMES

David Chura

I.

Time bomb.
That's how you describe it.

I'd prefer something prettier, gentler:
slash of birch across pinescape,
smudge of copper beech
on green mirror of maples.

But it's your cancer.
You name it.
Time bomb.
Locked away.
Your body,
case for its own
destruction.

II.

I must've known all along
you were a time bomb:
I picked my way through
childhood's minefield,
awed by your hair-triggered rage.

Now finally with this naming
I understand.
You were always your own ruin,
this small, final fuse set in you
long before I was born.

III.

It's your cancer.
You name it.
Time Bomb.
In naming it,
dare it to explode.
All you ask,
no one else taken.
Just you.
Alone.
Clean kill.

IV.

But it never is.
We both know and never say:
I will be the one left
to tweeze the shards of your sadness and rage
as they work their way
up through memory's bruised skin.

Or perhaps at my days' end
I'll have your courage
to name my demise,
to melt those scraps of mourning
into medals worn proudly,
to finally declare myself
soldier, veteran,
your son,
survivor of our war.

THE RAISING OF LAZARUS

Lucille Clifton

the dead shall rise again
whoever say
dust must be dust
don't see the trees
smell rain
remember africa
everything that goes
can come
stand up
even the dead shall rise

THE DEAD

Billy Collins

The dead are always looking down on us, they say,
while we are putting on our shoes or making a sandwich,
they are looking down through the glass-bottom boats of heaven
as they row themselves slowly through eternity.

They watch the tops of our heads moving below on earth,
and when we lie down in a field or on a couch,
drugged perhaps by the hum of a warm afternoon,
they think we are looking back at them,

which makes them lift their oars and fall silent
and wait, like parents, for us to close our eyes.

TRANSIENTS

Deborah Gordon Cooper

We are just passing through
these bones,
the way this wind
inhabits the ravine,
the way this light, in its
allotted time, illuminates
the hollow.

We are just passing through
these bones,
folding and opening
these limbs.

We work these hands,
making our sandwiches
and love;
look out at one another
from these faces,
watch a raven
trace the sky.

VISITATIONS

Deborah Gordon Cooper

On Tuesday
in the produce aisle,
choosing my oranges by feel
and by their fragrance,
I hear my father
whistling in my ear.
A Scottish lullaby.
Everything else stops.

There is a tenderness no border can contain.
A web that may be glimpsed
in certain, unexpected plays of light,
or felt
like a shawl
across one's shoulders
laid by unseen hands.

There are sounds in other decibels
the heart can hear
when the wind is right
and the mind has quieted its clicking.
The border guards are sleeping
at their stations.
Spirits come and go.

The wall between the living and the dead
is as yielding as a membrane,
is as porous as a skin.
Lay your palm against it

and you can hear their voices
in your hand
and in the place where the chest opens
like a flower.

They are not far away,
no farther than the breath
and enter us as easily,
in pine and peonies,
in oranges and rain.

Se Me Olividó Otra Vez

Eduardo C. Corral

after Donald Justice

I sit in bed, from the linen your scent still rises.
You're asleep inside your old guitar.

A mariachi suit draped on a chair, its copper buttons,
the eyes of jaguars stalking the night.

I sit in bed, from the linen your scent still rises.

Through a window a full moon brings to mind Borges,
there is such loneliness in that gold.

You're asleep inside your old guitar.

Are your calloused heels scraping its curved wood or
are there mice scurrying in the walls?

I sit in bed, from the linen your scent still rises.

I flick on a lamp, yellow light strikes your guitar
like dirt thrown on a coffin.

You're asleep inside your old guitar.
I sit in bed, from the linen your scent still rises.

REQUIEM

Barbara Crooker

for Judy

It is early March, each day a little bit greener,
crocus and snowdrops already in bloom, daffodils
sending up the tips of their spears.
When summer comes, we will take you to the river,
trickle your ashes through our fingers.
You will return to us in rain and snow,
season after season, roses, daisies, asters,
chrysanthemums. Wait for us on the other side.
The maple trees let go their red-gold leaves in fall;
in spring, apple blossoms blow to the ground
in the slightest breeze, a dusting of snow.
Let our prayers lift you, small and fine as they are,
like the breath of a sleeping baby. There is never
enough time. It runs through our fingers like water
in a stream. How many springs are enough,
peepers calling in the swamps? How many firefly-spangled
summers? Your father is waiting on the river bank,
he has two fishing poles and is baiting your hook.
Cross over, fish are rising to the surface,
a great blue heron stalks in the cattails,
the morning mist is rising, and the sun is breaking
through. Go, and let our hearts be broken.
We will not forget you.

HOME

Florence Chard Dacey

Now my sister, who is often right,
says the word my mother uttered at the end, when her eyes opened
and her rattling breath calmed, was
    Home.

We should have taken her home to die, my sister says.
She's sure that's what it meant.

My mother's higher brain was gone, the experts told us.
Five days into a coma, five days on morphine and water, while we waited.
Where did this word come from, the sound from her dry lips?

I want to think of this word arising through centuries
of Irish peat and German woods, a cradled word, a bed.

I want this word to have been fashioned over merry flame
and rehearsed in cathedrals, then uttered daily for millennium
so it arrives there, on her ninety-one-year-old lips
not as a simple plea or hope
but as her best pronouncement:

> *Home*, the flesh, hers and ours, the fire and water she meant to birth.

> *Home*, the house she made a village.

> *Home*, the lodging old and new, the grave, the dear auspicious end of
> wandering.

GUEST OF HONOR

Philip Dacey

Every day, I drive by the grave
of my fiancee's father.
She lost him when she was one.
He's our intimate stranger,

our guardian angel,
floating a la Chagall
just above our heads.
I go to him for love-lessons.

He touches my hand
with that tenderness
the dead have for the living.
When I touch her hand so,

she knows where I've been.
At the wedding,
he'll give her away to me.
And the glass he'll raise to toast us

will be a chalice brimful of sun,
his words heard all the more clearly
for their absence, as stone
is cut away to form dates.

RESURRECTION, OR WHAT HE TOLD ME TO DO WHEN HE DIED

Todd Davis

Take me to the field where the river runs
by the swamp. Dig a hole deep enough
that dogs and coyotes won't dine on
what's left. Place cedar boughs
beneath my head, cover my body with ash
from the fireplace, dirt from the garden.
Spread seed here and there in no particular
pattern. Don't visit until warmth comes back
into the earth and spring rains move on. Then
see how jewelweed sprouts from my chest
and clover climbs from my eyes.

SHIFTING THE SUN

Diana Der-Hovanessian

When your father dies, say the Irish,
you lose your umbrella against bad weather.
May his sun be your light, say the Armenians.

When your father dies, say the Welsh,
you sink a foot deeper into the earth.
May you inherit his light, say the Armenians.

When your father dies, say the Canadians,
you run out of excuses.
May you inherit his sun, say the Armenians.

When your father dies, say the Indians,
he comes back as the thunder.
May you inherit his light, say the Armenians.

When your father dies, say the Russians,
he takes your childhood with him.
May you inherit his light say the Armenians.

When your father dies, say the British,
you join his club you vowed you wouldn't.
May you inherit his sun, say the Armenians.

When your father dies, say the Armenians,
your sun shifts forever
and you walk in his light.

To My Father

Blaga Dimitrova

You gathered incredible strength
in order to die
to seem calm and fully conscious
without complaint, without trembling
without a cry
so that I would not be afraid

Your wary hand
slowly grew cold in mine
and guided me carefully
beyond into the house of death
so I might come to know it

Thus in the past you used to take my hand
and guide me through the world
and show me life
so I would not fear

I will follow after you
confident as a child
toward the silent country
where you went first
so I would not feel a stranger there

And I would not be afraid.

Star Light, Star Bright

W. D. Ehrhart

Under stars in late October cold
you asked, if stars are suns,
why is ours much bigger than the rest.
I said, because they're far away.
As far away as Grammy's house, you asked.
Farther still, I said, much farther.
Where is Grammy now, you asked.
Her body's in the ground, I said,
but maybe what she really was
is up there somewhere shining down
like starlight you and I can feel
all around us on a night like this.
You stood in silence for awhile,
gazing up, one thoughtful hand
resting lightly on my shoulder,
one stretched out and turned palm up
as if to catch the starlight.
Then you said, almost singing,
       what a pretty feeling
         to be a little star,
           white, and beautiful.
I could feel the whole heart of you
lifting dreams beyond the reach
of earthbound limitations and I
love you more than you will know
until I'm starlight and you understand
how each of us needs little stars

to lift our dreams beyond ourselves,
and I was hers, and you were mine.

Kaddish

Alan Elyshevitz

  for Rose Dorn

May His Great Name be sanctified
by the sweet cheap sodas
you bought me and my brothers
from the laundromat vending machine
along with forbidden diner BLTs
created according to His will. *Omein*

Blessed, praised, glorified, exalted, extolled, honored, elevated,
lauded —
His Name and your name,
and the one name you called us —
"Sweetie" this, "Sweetie" that —
for you could never remember
your grandchildren's names.

Blessings, hymns, praise, consolation
for the grease monkeys half your age
who flirted with you at the Olds dealership
where you kept the books upon which
all of them suckled. *Omein*

Why, after selling our grandfather's car,
did you live in front of the Magnavox
with the twisted antenna that snared
Guy Lombardo on New Year's Eve
while you sniffed your dead husband's
dead smoke rings?

Why did you never marry after 1959?
This is His secret, His secret and yours,
which you carried with you to the Bingo hall,
to the diner and the laundromat,
to successful hip surgery
and not so successful treatment of
heart
bladder
spleen
skin
heart
kidneys
heart
lungs
heart heart heart

Blessed be the white wisps of your hair
and the coma that subdued your fear —
that ugly tube-tied restfulness
that masquerades as death. *Omein*

Now that you rest in your House of Israel
made of pine, we stand with a sweating rabbi
and his minion of flies in the crux of summer,
dust in our collars, rivers in our palms,
the dry taste of prayer on our lips.

Yis'ga'dal v'yis'kadash
The least we can do
is stand for you, stand
forever and ever. *Omein*

AUTUMN

Teresa Boyle Falsani

Like Keats, I welcome Autumn this year,
having spent the summer watching my father die,
his limbs waste and wither,
eyes cloud the sun,
words fade to silence,
heart slow to final freeze.
Now, November feigns a replay—
grasses bow like supplicants,
the peeper chorus quiets in the reeds.
Morning frost pools in the hollows,
ice on the lake reflects
indifference in the sky.

Come, bleak November.
Do your worst.
I can live buried in snow,
get along without green,
even eye with patience
your pale deceitful sun,
the way we lie fallow in grief,
gather will to plant again
fields winnowed of our dead.

STILL BIRTH: A PSALM FOR HOLY WEEK

Mara Faulkner, OSB

for Rowan Elizabeth b. and d. Feb. 2, 1998

1. *"Sing to the Lord a new song."*

the secret of your becoming
        burned down to a handful of ash
                in a little wooden box
                                meant to hold music
now you must be the intricate workings
        the far off melody
                beginning
                       ending
                       beginning

2. *"Even the sparrow finds a home."*

little bird
        unfledged
                come twisted from the egg
                without the chance to sing
                        in the branchy tree
                                of this family

3. *"Let the desert rejoice and bloom."*

rowan—mountain ash
                taking root in the prairie
                    the northwoods
your delicate leaves shadowing
                all the days ahead

on all our nights

        your berries

            an ineffaceable mark

4. *"Let the children come to me and do not hinder them."*

a son

    young and slim as a flute

    was lately learning to be a father

        humming tunes

            to your ears

                uncoiling in the womb

now he weeps in his mother's arms

for you've gone beyond the sound of his songs

    carrying

        small as you are

            the weight of his dreams

5. *"You have knit me together in my mother's womb."*

she was making a sweater of bluegreen wool

        like the hills

        the sea

          around Galway

    the twining cables

    the cryptic spirals

        all unwilling to say with certainty

          where the

beginning is

          where the end

but her clever hands

    couldn't help you

    trying to knit yourself in the dark

        the strands a

knotted tangle

                                        the ancient pattern gone
             hopelessly awry

        6. *"God gives the barren woman a home."*

i want to howl like a wolf
             like a blizzard wind tearing
                                        the roofs
                                                  from unbroken houses
                  scouring
                        the land
                              to rock

high-pitched   raw-throated
             an Irish mother whose only child
                                        is lost in a cold north sea
but my mouth is sewn shut
and the cries burrow
                        down
                              and down
for i'm not your mother
             your grandmother
i'm only a maiden aunt
        the surge of milk in futile breasts
        arms closing on empty air
                        what can i know
                                        about loss?

        7. *"What we will become has not yet been revealed."*

knowing the wild untrammeled freedom
                                        of viruses
                                        and renegade chromosomes
             who would be so greedy of pain
                              as to start loving early?
we all did—foolish family!

during the long nine months
       hands curved to receive the flutter
                   of small fingers
stiff arms rounded into cradles
tongues grew supple practicing comfort and silly nicknames
imaginations
          warm   dark   blood-rich
                 fashioned hands and hair
                   feet that could dance
                fashioned a future

what will happen to this family
               now bereft of lighthearted hope—
   will we plant trees
       the trees coax birds
       our arms
       our wooden tongues
              learn solace and shade
   will we be steadfast for this infinite time
       refusing to be distracted
             from the labor
             of giving birth
                 to grief?

WITH STARS

Tess Gallagher

> *for M.K.*

My mother speaks from the dark—why
haven't I closed my eyes? Why don't I
sleep? And when I say I can't, she
wraps the quilt around me and leads me
to the window. I am four years old and
a star has the power of wishes.
We stare out together, but she sees past
their fierce shimmering sameness, each
point of light the emblem
of some lost, remembered face. What
do they want? I ask. "Not to be
forgotten," she says, and draws me close.
Then her gaze sifts the scattered brilliance.
Her hand goes out—"There! that one!" so
her own mother, dead years back, looks down
on us. Sleep then like a hammer
among the orbiting dead.

Tonight it is the stars reminding
keeps me up past midnight.
My mother's voice, as in that childhood room,
is with me so surely I might rush out
and find that window, those stars
no further than the next doorway, and her
there waiting—awake all night
because I was awake. "Go

to sleep," I'd say. "They want me
awake tonight." And she'd know who I meant—
those others still living and afar
because I think them there. And why not
give the dead this benefit of separations?
There were so many nameless before.
But oh, if one falls, *if*—
how can that child ever fall asleep
until sunrise?

FUNERAL

Jane Graham George

on this tempest day
low cloud at my chest
and footfall heavy
as a workhorse
through frost-charred bluestem
the lake its own opposite
earth-brown mottled
as a salamander's back
all but frozen
eight swans
white but not yet cold
single file
in the narrow ring
of open water
like gondolas
the season of short days
thunder of an ice age
knowing the gray
shades purgatorial & cleansing
ashy coneheads
bowing now in prayer

LIFE AFTER DEATH

Laura Gilpin

These things I know:
    How the living go on living
    and how the dead go on living with them
so that in a forest
    even a dead tree casts a shadow
    and the leaves fall one by one
and the branches break in the wind
and the bark peels off slowly
and the trunk cracks
    and the rain seeps in through the cracks

and the trunk falls to the ground
and the moss covers it
    and in the spring the rabbits find it
and build their nest
inside the dead tree
so that nothing is wasted in nature
    or in love.

AFTER

Linda Glaser

When they lowered you
into raw sharp-edged earth,
the realness
caved in all around me
gasping, breathless.

You are gone.

Ripped from countless
hidden places,
the roots of a beloved tree
yanked down by a storm,
exposed and useless.

All darkness
the all-consuming absence.
Nothing will ever be the same.

And yet,
in time,
softly,
softly,
like babies' feet,
like spring itself
after vacant winter,
you return.

From backstage corners
you make small appearances
now and then.

Blessedly mundane moments
light my heart
with the vibrant flesh of memory.

At times, my heart speaks to you.
At times, you answer.

At times, the tears insist
you are gone.

Unalterably gone.

But the realness of your life
still breathes inside me.
You have altered our world.
And you still do.
I see you in new ways.
I grow. I learn from you.

You are still present
somehow,
in this great Oneness,
a beloved blessing,
firmly planted
among all those
known and unknown,
whom you have touched
or will somehow still touch.

And the garden of your life
continues to grow.

SHARING GRIEF

Jane Ellen Glasser

We pass it back and forth
through telephone wires.
We divide it
into boxes—
yours, mine.
We compare the forms it takes
in the foreign countries
inside us.
Each day it is different;
each day it is the same.
Together,
we plant rocks.
Together,
we throw out
the empty hooks
of interrogatives:
Why *her* and not another?
Why not *us*?
Why like *that*?
Not "Why," time teaches us,
but "Is." If death is
nothing
but the end
of the accident of living,
we must learn to let go
of the universe
spinning a hole in our palms.

Harmonium

Vicki Graham

I.

All day the wind blows colorless
from the river, wearing stone,
bridge, trees, to monotone.

Arrows on a weather map
can't chart this city's wind
as it wraps cars and buildings,

then fills the branches
of the sycamores edging the parkway
and lifts the water in hard points.

II.

Firecat. Hemlock. Jar:
word by word she feels her way
through fictions that ricochet

and coil, spiral from the page
in girandoles. *What syllable
are you seeking*, she wants to ask her mother.

What sleep? What sleep?
But she has turned away from them;
nothing can wake her now.

III.

At dusk, the wind fell,
and when her mother died,

the room was still. Day
thinned to a white line

over New Jersey, and the river
flattened to poured steel.

IV.

Loss tunes the body, tightens
its sinews the way wind

pulls the marsh grass taut.
The voice loses color; lucent,

bound to a single chord, it hums
to itself. Only bone in the wind

could sound this note;
only bare trees could hold it.

AFTERGLOW

Marj Hahne

A man asks his wife, disappearing
in a hospital bed, to call home once
more, leave a message on the machine
so he will always have her
voice when she's gone.
                              Her voice
         played, played
again will be something
like light from a star
dead for who-knows-how-many light
years from its own swallowed air—
                                        what's left
is black and splendor, a glimmer reaching out
to the living.
                    Something
like their first night, all
body and liquid and vapor—
the spark, flash lasting
long after the collapse.

EAGLE POEM

Joy Harjo

To pray you open your whole self
To sky, to earth, to sun, to moon
To one whole voice that is you.
And know there is more
That you can't see, can't hear
Can't know except in moments
Steadily growing, and in languages
That aren't always sound but other
Circles of motion.
Like eagle that Sunday morning
Over Salt River. Circled in blue sky
In wind, swept our hearts clean
With sacred wings.
We see you, see ourselves and know
That we must take the utmost care
And kindness in all things.
Breathe in, knowing we are made of
All this, and breathe, knowing
We are truly blessed because we
Were born, and die soon, within a
True circle of motion,
Like eagle rounding out the morning
Inside us.
We pray that it will be done
In beauty.
In beauty.

SOME YEARS

Penny Harter

Some years, my father made a garden
along the creek out back, carried
topsoil from the woods that crept
to our yard's edge, cut sticks for vines,
and made the creek's edge ripen
with pole beans, wax beans,
floppy heads of lettuce, and tomatoes
that burst like planets from green clouds.

I don't remember when the houses came
to take the fields and woods behind our house,
to tame the creek into a culvert where it lost
the clay we used to scoop from its gray banks,
the turtles, and the tadpoles that we trapped
in jars of silted water—and then let go.

But I know that's when my father
gave up on the garden, seeded his lawn
like all the rest, though he sometimes stood
where it had been, listening for wind
in trees that were no more,
and the song of running water.

Today as I think of his ashes
neatly packaged on my closet shelf
waiting to join my mother's
in the family plot,

I honor his garden, wanting
to dig up the grass and find good soil again,
then let it crumble through my fingers
as I gently give him back
to what he lost.

A BREEZE BENDS THE GRASSES...

Margaret Hasse

the kind my father picked
and brought to his lips to blow
the sound of a startled bird—

the cry his heart must have made
when he drove himself far
from us time and again.

Teach me, teach me
to make music
from plain grass.

Father showed me the way
to stretch a blade between thumbs,
to whistle a lone note.

He said: *That's it! Good,*
coaching me to climb a scale,
hit high notes,

practicing a melody
of happiness
he could not compose.

Why did I think all these years
only of how he was distant,
then disappeared,

and not of how he placed
his hands around mine
praying with me a green song?

T'AI CHI CHIH PRACTICE

Naomi Haugen
   after "Morning Poem" by Mary Oliver

   each pond with its blazing lilies
   is a prayer heard and answered
   lavishly
   every morning —Mary Oliver

every morning
I step
in patterns
slow and ancient

unload
my suitcase of grief
unpack
my trunk of despair
and touch the silent water.

with bare feet on carpet
I carry my arms
in parallel arcs
hold the invisible globe

of my sadness
and allow the crust
of fitful nights
to soften.

my teacher has said —
the souls of your feet
are a bubbling well —

I have learned to name

and form each movement:
daughter in the valley
daughter on the mountaintop
passing clouds —

On days when my feet
find no water
my hair flutters
in the breeze

of the mortician's
gurney, passing
over and over
through this room

as if the dying
cannot stop —
but if the day
begins to show

its colors
and if the wind
tames itself
and settles

in the branches
above my head
my feet find
their wings

and like Mercury
I fly to the pond
stir the waters
of morning

and pass my weight
lavishly
from flower
to blazing flower

SOMEWHERE SAFE TO SEA

Susan Carol Hauser

> *Even the weariest river*
> *winds somewhere safe to sea.* —Charles Swinburne

Duluth, May 12, 2002
Gooseberry Falls

It is not much comfort—to think
of you at sea, returned
to the water, or the air,

whatever that land is
that we seem to come from.

It is hard, though, to not
indulge in metaphor:

the rivers of our blood
returning again and again
to the heart;

rain, snow, mist,
even ice returning again
and again to the ocean.

I turn to water, then,
to waterfalls,
on this the anniversary
of your passing, perhaps
with hope of finding you,
falling into grace,
into the quiet water

that down the way nudges
into Lake Superior, resisting
the waves that resist the current,

where I skip stones,
small memories,
and pocket one pebble
for when I am lost,
as though at sea.

REFLECTION

Susan Carol Hauser

The lake is quiet
this afternoon,
bereft of wind,

even of breeze,

the blue of the sky
laid out
on the surface;

the heavens then
beneath our feet,

we steer the canoe
as though by stars,

reaching with our paddles
for the sweet, dark deep,

pulling hard
against this life,
against death,

until the celestial waters
open to us

and the wake murmurs
our names.

JARDÍN DE PAZ

Lorraine Healy

I do not visit his louvered house,
where the family keeps pace
with life. Instead, I go
to his other house, a plain
slab of granite set in grass.
The rectangular shape of his sleep
sunk a little lower each time
as his body goes. It takes
a steeling of the sternum to kneel down
but then my hand finds its way
to his name, caressing the stone,
the last skin of my father's.
I tell it the news and call it Dad—my fingers
absent-minded in the grooves of the dates
when he was here and ours.

I make slow friends
with this quiet place, this corner
by the nameless red bush,
the tidy silence, the green
grids of those we lost.
Isn't it all a bit too circumspect
for you? I ask him. No one answers.
My father would have laughed.
But now? Has he acquired
the gravity of the dead?
And inch by inch the soil that covers him
compacts upon what's left,
rain bathing the helpless bones.

ALZHEIMER'S

Bob Hicok

Chairs move by themselves, and books.
Grandchildren visit, stand
new and nameless, their faces' puzzles
missing pieces. She's like a fish

in deep ocean, its body made of light.
She floats through rooms, through
my eyes, an old woman bereft
of chronicle, the parable of her life.

And though she's almost a child
there's still blood between us:
I passed through her to arrive.
So I protect her from knives,

stairs, from the street that calls
as rivers do, a summons to walk away,
to follow. And dress her,
demonstrate how buttons work,

when she sometimes looks up
and says my name, the sound arriving
like the trill of a bird so rare
it's rumored no longer to exist.

Letting Go of What Cannot be Held Back

Bill Holm

Let go of the dead now.
The rope in the water,
the cleat on the cliff,
do them no good anymore.
Let them fall, sink, go away,
become invisible as they tried
so hard to do in their own dying.
We needed to bother them
with what we called help.
We were the needy ones.
The dying do their own work with
tidiness, just the right speed,
sometimes even a little
satisfaction. So quiet down.
Let them go. Practice
your own song. Now.

DREAM

Paul Hostovsky

You're alive and riding your bicycle
to school and I am worried about you
riding your bicycle all the way to school
so I get in my car and drive like a maniac
through the dream over curbs and lawns
sideswiping statuary and birdbaths along
the way frantically seeking you everywhere
the rear wheel of your bicycle disappearing
around the next corner and the next and then
I am riding a bicycle too and sounding
the alarm which sounds like a bicycle bell
so no one believes it's an alarm and I pedal
faster and faster my knees bumping up against
the handlebars which by now have sprouted
ribbons with pompoms and a basket attached
with your lunch inside and I'm pedaling to save
my life and your life and finally when I find you
in the dream you aren't dead yet you're alive
and a little angry and embarrassed to see me
all out of breath on a girl's bicycle holding
your lunch out in my hand trembling with joy

KADDISH

David Ignatow

Mother of my birth, for how long were we together
in your love and my adoration of your self?
For the shadow of a moment as I breathed your pain
and you breathed my suffering, as we knew
of shadows in lit rooms that would swallow the light.

Your face beneath the oxygen tent was alive
but your eyes were closed. Your breathing was hoarse
but your sleep was with death. I was alone with you
as it was when I was young but only alone now
and not with you. I was to be alone forever
as I was learning, watching you become alone.

Earth is your mother as you were mine, my earth,
my sustenance, my comfort and my strength
and now without you I turn to your mother
and seek from her that I may meet you again
in rock and stone: whisper to the stone,
I love you; whisper to the rock, I found you;
whisper to earth, Mother, I have found my mother
and I am safe and always have been.

First Call of Spring Among the Frogs

Janet Jerve

in memory of my father

The mist hangs low
and summons the monks
to circle the water—
the leader's ohm
signals the others
to join.

What is the name
for comfort
when two dissonant notes
sound like one?

They say
your father is gone
he is here.

YAHRZEIT

Sheila Golburgh Johnson

Each
anniversary
of your death
I burn a candle in
a glass to celebrate
the annual progress
of your soul to heaven.
I'm not much on heaven
but I know your soul.
I remember watching it depart,
your body strained and laboring
as it labored fifty years ago
to bring me forth to joy.
Now you return, a golden flame
so delicate my slightest breath
causes you to flicker
and threaten to
depart
again

When the Dead Come to Visit in Dreams

Deborah Keenan

They have questions about placement.
"Where have you assigned me? How many memories are left?"
My father asks if I remember his early beauty.
He asks, "Are you happy?" but is gone before I can think
of the answer he wants, the answer I have.

In the first dream he sleeps in his bed.
My mother sends me in to wake him, I cup my small hand
around the curve of his shoulder, I touch his breathing
waist, I call, "Dad, Dad, it's time to wake up,"
but he sleeps on. I put my mouth to his dreaming ear
and say good-bye.

My mother, standing in the doorframe of the same dream
tells me to take his car and leave. Driving away
in my father's white Studebaker I am so happy. I call
back over my shoulder to say, "Yes, I'm happy,"
then remember the question comes from another dream.

My friend asks if I'm famous, if I've had more children.
When I tell her—another son—she says in her dream voice,
"I hope the new one is quiet. You need some quiet."

When the dead come to visit in dreams they are deeply curious
but disinterested in some holy, unexpected ways.
Most times it doesn't matter what I answer. I can say,
"You're an angel in my sky." I can say, "Dad, I miss you."

I can tell them all this while I'm dreaming, or

on the freeway the next morning, frost past the danger point,
the road a collective illusion. I tell them
I love them. I tell them anything I want.

When the dead come to visit me at night they take some part
of my heart away, as if it's part of some celestial puzzle
they are working on, but they always
bring my heart back to me, and I wake up
lonely, and relieved by their absence.

LET EVENING COME

Jane Kenyon

Let the light of late afternoon
shine through chinks in the barn, moving
up the bales as the sun moves down.

Let the crickets take up chafing
as a woman takes up her needles
and her yarn. Let evening come.

Let dew collect on the hoe abandoned
in long grass. Let the stars appear
and the moon disclose her silver horn.

Let the fox go back to its sandy den.
Let the wind die down. Let the shed
go black inside. Let evening come.

To the bottle in the ditch, to the scoop
in the oats, to air in the lung
let evening come.

Let it come, as it will, and don't
be afraid. God does not leave us
comfortless, so let evening come.

NAMING

C. L. Knight

If I name this grief,
define it
with guilt
and redemption,
call it drowning,
desolation,
call it
fire and stone,

then I am bound
to care for it,
like a stray cat I name,
that demands I feed him.
He comes and goes,
sometimes disappears
for days and then returns,
insisting that
I remember.

FATHER

Ted Kooser

May 19, 1999

Today you would be ninety-seven
if you had lived, and we would all be
miserable, you and your children,
driving from clinic to clinic,
an ancient, fearful hypochondriac
and his fretful son and daughter,
asking directions, trying to read
the complicated, fading map of cures.
But with your dignity intact
you have been gone for twenty years,
and I am glad for all of us, although
I miss you every day—the heartbeat
under your necktie, the hand cupped
on the back of my neck, Old Spice
in the air, your voice delighted with stories.
On this day each year you loved to relate
that at the moment of your birth
your mother glanced out the window
and saw lilacs in bloom. Well, today
lilacs are blooming in side yards
all over Iowa, still welcoming you.

MOTHER

Ted Kooser

Mid April already, and the wild plums
bloom at the roadside, a lacy white
against the exuberant, jubilant green
of new grass and the dusty, fading black
of burned-out ditches. No leaves, not yet,
only the delicate, star-petaled
blossoms, sweet with their timeless perfume.

You have been gone a month today
and have missed three rains and one nightlong
watch for tornadoes. I sat in the cellar
from six to eight while fat spring clouds
went somersaulting, rumbling east. Then it poured,
a storm that walked on legs of lightning,
dragging its shaggy belly over the fields.

The meadowlarks are back, and the finches
are turning from green to gold. Those same
two geese have come to the pond again this year,
honking in over the trees and splashing down.
They never nest, but stay a week or two
then leave. The peonies are up, the red sprouts
burning in circles like birthday candles,

for this is the month of my birth, as you know,
the best month to be born in, thanks to you,
everything ready to burst with living.
There will be no more new flannel nightshirts
sewn on your old black Singer, no birthday card

addressed in a shaky but businesslike hand.
You asked me if I would be sad when it happened

and I am sad. But the iris I moved from your house
now hold in the dusty dry fists of their roots
green knives and forks as if waiting for dinner,
as if spring were a feast. I thank you for that.
Were it not for the way you taught me to look
at the world, to see the life at play in everything,
I would have to be lonely forever.

HOW IT IS

Maxine Kumin

Shall I say how it is in your clothes?
A month after your death I wear your blue jacket.
The dog at the center of my life recognizes
you've come to visit, he's ecstatic.
In the left pocket, a hole.
In the right, a parking ticket
delivered up last August on Bay State Road.
In my heart, a scatter like milkweed,
a flinging from the pods of the soul.
My skin presses your old outline.
It is hot and dry inside.

I think of the last day of your life,
old friend, how I would unwind it, paste
it together in a different collage,
back from the death car idling in the garage,
back up the stairs, your praying hands unlaced,
reassembling the bits of bread and tuna fish
into a ceremony of sandwich,
running the home movie backward to a space
we could be easy in, a kitchen place
with vodka and ice, our words like living meat.

Dear friend, you have excited crowds
with your example. They swell
like wine bags, straining at your seams.
It will be years gathering up our words,
fishing out letters, snapshots, stains,

leaning my ribs against this durable cloth
to put on the dumb blue blazer of your death.

Candles in April

Julie Landsman

Gold flame hallows April dawn
as two candles burn my parents' deaths
two days two years apart.

In this Jewish light, gift from my husband,
I see my mother, my father
just before their bones powdered:
easy arm-in-arm walk,
climbing up from their garden
proud of bursting stalks of corn,
tomatoes that managed
to cling to a stony hill in Connecticut.

Do not forget me, his candle says,
I am still drifting through your world
caught in the voice of Louis Armstrong,
at your favorite morning coffee shop
or on the lavender breeze of lilac that will come late this year.

Among pictures you rarely bring out, I am there, her candle says,
in a white satin dress waiting for your father
who wears a cream colored suit for our wedding day
just before he returned to fly his beloved Corsairs
and before the war in the blue green Pacific.

I am there in the flame of my anger, he says,
when you came home from marching deep into the south,
after the hot train ride to Montgomery and the yellow daffodils

by the side of the road all the way through
Virginia, Georgia, Mississippi to Alabama.

I am here in my silence, she says,
as the flame dwindles in its clear glass.
Imagine my love, underneath all those unspoken years.

These days of Yahrzeit,
I am hallowed, carved down to
darkness, love.

DEATH OF A BEST FRIEND

Charlene Langfur

I don't know how to write of passing.

Of the rough edges, how it blanches all of a world.
Nothing escapes it.

Not the green grass, the air in the morning, the thick summer shrubs fat
with life.

No praise takes to it. No encomiums. No poet's phrase.

A strange sense of density is left.
And earthquakes inside a body,
sudden eerie trembling
seismic but not.

The only way out is through the bramble forward, evident life,
into blue mechanical joy without any float or lift to it
no yawl or drive or drift or sentience

only pitch and dross
the there and the not there of joy

and the hours like minions

everything is there but you are not there,
rare angel of mine, life's is.

HAVE YOU PRAYED

Li-Young Lee

When the wind
turns and asks me, in my father's voice,
Have you prayed?

I know three things. One:
I'm never finished answering to the dead.

Two: A man is four winds and three fires.
And the four winds are his father's voice,
his mother's voice. . .

Or maybe he's seven winds and ten fires.
And the fires are seeing, hearing, touching,
dreaming, thinking. . .
Or is he the breath of God?

When the wind turns traveler
and asks, in my father's voice, *Have you prayed?*
I remember three things.
One: A father's love

is milk and sugar,
two-thirds worry, two-thirds grief, and what's left over

is trimmed and leavened to make the bread
the dead and the living share.

And patience? That's to endure
the terrible leavening and kneading.

And wisdom? That's my father's face in sleep.

When the wind
asks, *Have you prayed?*
I know it's only me

reminding myself
a flower is one station between
earth's wish and earth's rapture, and blood

was fire, salt, and breath long before
it quickened any wand or branch, any limb
that woke speaking. It's just me

in the gowns of the wind,
or my father through me, asking,
Have you found your refuge yet?
asking, *Are you happy?*

Strange. A troubled father. A happy son.
The wind with a voice. And me talking to no one.

BETWEEN THE WORDS

Vicky Lettmann

in memory of Deb Shelton

You have gone into the pauses of our conversation
the time beyond time and time within time

you are in those moments when we sit in the audience
waiting for the curtain to rise

and the end when the curtain has closed
and the actors have taken their bows

you are within the pauses of the bird's song
when we strain to hear the next note

in the water between the fish
in the traveler's silence within a foreign language

you are in the air that fills the sky
in the moments after the sunset

you are between night and day
spirit next to soul

years next to laughter
you are in the space between the words

the connecting air around periods and commas
the moment before the artist picks up her brush

THE CHANGE

Denise Levertov

For years the dead
were the terrible weight of their absence,
the weight of what one had not put in their hands.
Rarely a visitation—dream or vision—
lifted that load for a moment, like someone
standing behind one and briefly taking
the heft of a frameless pack.
But the straps remained, and the ache—
though you can learn not to feel it
except when malicious memory
pulls downward with sudden force.
Slowly there comes a sense
that for some time the burden
has been what you need anyway.
How flimsy to be without it, ungrounded, blown
hither and thither, colliding with stern solids.
And then they begin to return, the dead:
but not as visions. They're not
separate now, not to be seen, no
it's they who see: they displace,
for seconds, for minutes, maybe longer,
the mourner's gaze with their own. Just now,
that shift of light, arpeggio
on ocean's harp—
not the accustomed bearer
of heavy absence saw it, it was perceived
by the long-dead, long absent, looking
out from within one's wideopen eyes.

BEAR BUTTE PASSAGE

Eric Lochridge

Rose light on buffalo grass
calls you from the room.
So, father, you slip past the weeping
ring of family at that heavy bed

to gaze on lush swirls of coneflower,
Indian paintbrush and big bluestem
bathed in unearthly dusk all the way
to the slumbering hulk of the butte.

Barefoot on the baroque prairie,
you head north, toward clarity,
no longer confounded by fence, foothill
or the mind that failed you.

At last, the bear awakes and lifts you
onto its pine-stippled shoulder
to keep that last lavender sunset in sight.

Reconsidering the Enlightenment

Donna J. Long

for Barbara Joan Long 1935-1985

The technician says try not to move.
You still those parts you can.
What you cannot touch scatters,
bursts in the onslaught of x-ray.
Those cells replicating a prison

you will leave long before me.
I touch you until your skin and bones
might break, talk to your breathing
body, finally I watch over you.
How long this idleness will hold

my throat, a pheasant in a Lab's jaws. Years
later I lay awake, held still by a heavy comforter
against the winter's dark window, and find
the hum of one night traveler after another
synchronizing a perfect wedge of sound

across the glass, a slow note
reaching crescendo at the center
then fading north or south. In between
the steady work of my own breathing.
I wonder at it all: how sound becomes

music in the space of the pane, how
the pheasant's feathers kaleidoscope, vivid
beyond its last breath, how

this millennia of mutation creates
our capacity for wonder and for grief.

GIRLFRIEND

Audre Lorde

March 27, 1990

It's almost a year and I still
can't deal with you
not being
at the end of the line.

I read your name in memorial poems
and think they must be insane
mistaken malicious
in terrible error
just plain wrong

not that there haven't been times before
months passing madly sadly
we not speaking
> *get off my case, will you please?*
> *oh, just lighten up!*

But I can't get you out
of my hair my spirit
my special hotline phone book
is this what it means to live
forever when will I
not miss picking up the receiver
after a pregnancy of silence
one of us born again
with a brand-new address or poem
miffed

because the other doesn't jump
at the sound
of her beloved voice?

SWEDISH RYE

Christina Lovin

What is it that I fear to smear like grease
across the starched white apron
of this page? Memories that cling and prick
like caraway between the teeth:

my father singing in the kitchen
as he kneaded dark rye dough
across a wooden board,
his hands full of the mystery of yeast
and flour—full of Illinois prairie sun,
tan and firm—working gluten lumps
from the raw bread. Crusted toughly—
the loaves he formed—thick-skinned
and earthy. Hard to chew,
harder to swallow.

Last time I bent to kiss his head
the skin was crisp and brown,
a taste of salt rising on my lips,
taking me home only to leave me
an orphan in the empty kitchen,
the oven open-mouthed and cold.

GOLDENRODS

by Raymond Luczak

for Edward J. Luczak 1926 - 1989

Summers ago when we used to play hide-and-seek across the street,
its voluptuous boughs ganged up on us,
its gold powder smudging our arms. We ran too fast
sometimes, its stiff leaves scratching our legs;
how good it felt then to stand in a clearing,
where forget-me-nots and lazy-eyed susans led
way to a breeze tickling
our exposed legs. There we stood, rubbing
and waving off the mosquitoes. In time we came to ignore
those yellow things.
There were so many of them.

> *Years have passed; I have forgotten about them*
> *until now. I had never thought of them as*
> *weeds.*

They are still standing in the November winds,
brown-starved for a little more warmth. Their rickety stems are
now hollowed out from the creeping chill. Of course
they have endured all this before—they let fall
their seeds on the moist patches of the earth, sprouting
so many more like them. They stand silent
when dozens of their kind are trampled upon; they huddle together
amidst hailstorms and wreckages. They have
no other protection against their kind. They do not question
why, and never how else should they live. They are too busy
preparing for the next smothering of winter.

It occurs to me now they are stronger than we. They have been expecting all this. How much faith they hold in their own seeds.

ELEGY FOR A MAN AND A HOUSE

Marjorie Maddox

Everything in my voice: antique.
It cracks like the static of your sleep
the last time you rolled over,
away, curls into something older
than wood, frame, this empty square:
roof, door, a wall to measure
how and why we grow, windows
slit like an eye on the side of the moon
that caught us young, let go
before your breath dipped, stopped.
Oh, Giacomo, though it's winter
and this rough floor cold,
I walk with my shoes off
to catch your splinters.

The Grandfather Passes

Joanne McCarthy

for William Stafford

Grandfather, speak to us.
Tell us the earth's story
again, how wind sings
in the marsh, how black rocks
never soften. Tell us the
sound that a mountain makes
after the clear-cut, how
sky holds its breath, what the
brittle river says in winter.
Your words are stronger
than blackberry vines. They
cling to the truth and
worry it. Though your voice turn
to grass, we will listen.

Husband

Mary C. McCarthy

When you left me
darkness opened
up at my feet
and I froze
just where I was,
robbed of any
destination,
lonely as the man
in a space suit,
or the deep sea diver
who must carry all of his air
with him. I can't
come up too fast
or I will die of grief
blooming like a deadly gas
in my blood.
What is left here
anyway? The hills
rolled out flat
into deserts, the rivers
pulled back into the earth
leaving dry beds cracked
and crazed
like glazed china
hot from the kiln.
I will not bend.
I do not care
what rules I break.

I will stand here
and howl my loss
beneath the stony moon
until even you
will hear me.

CURE

Kathleen McGookey

Take the red sailboat out; plant the garden. Every summer, I do
something for the first time without my parents.

Every summer, I wash my mother's hair, comb my father's, help
them into clean pajamas . . . .

And after, a bird lands in my hand to eat seeds, then
pauses above me for the white feather in my fingers

and grief lifts a little, the bird bears it up,
swallow or chickadee or wren

and leaves a space . . . . my father's exhaled breath,
my mother's reflection, before the stone, before she went away—

THE WEIGHT

Ann McGovern

Objects remain.
Baskets bought in Borneo
the day we saw the deadly snake

on a river trip, coiled
in a jungle tree above us.
"You die before you scream," our guide said.

A Turkish rug from Istanbul. We looked
at a pile of hundreds. We might have curled up
on the bottom, smothered in history.

A Vietnamese medicine chest
I use for jewelry, one drawer
for the earrings you gave me.

How can I forget the countries where we bought them,
the shops and the shopkeepers,
the ways I thanked you for each lovely pair?

But mostly, your leg against mine,
for instance.
The shocking weight.

POTATOES

Ethna McKiernan

Someone is weeping in the kitchen.
It is my father, crying quietly
as he peels the dinner potatoes.
He pierces their white hearts with a fork
and steam rises upward toward his beard.
Below, hot tears salt the bowl.
The intimacy of the moment staggers,
as when I stumbled once, as a child,
upon him cupping my mother's face
in broad, noon daylight as they entered
the deep, private zone of a kiss.
How could he have known, when he made
that vow fifty-seven years ago,
how suddenly and readily she'd leave him —
pork chops burnt, potatoes blackening
over gas — for that thin stranger
called Alzheimer, waltzing through
the kitchen door like a suitor
who has never lost a single lover's hand
he's played?

CATALOGING MISTAKES

Erik K. Mortenson

and then there was the time her father died and she asked me where
I thought souls go afterwards and I said why do they have to go anywhere
maybe they die too and are finally at peace and what makes you think
we have a soul anyway maybe when we die we die and that's it and that's all
and sometimes dead is better and wasn't that true for him and then she just cried
harder than before but quieter and I knew she would the whole time
I was saying this but I couldn't stop myself I don't know what made me
think that would be helpful that it would actually be a comfort to her
I just couldn't say what she wanted like that souls go to heaven and watch
over us but even worse was what I never thought to say at all which was
that his soul was in the way she held her chin just there and in the curls of her
hair and the gold flecks in the blue of her eyes and in her mouth when she
peeled cut and ate a pear with a slim knife and her thumb and that his soul
was in her heart when she asked me the question in the first place

When I Am Asked

Lisel Mueller

When I am asked
how I began writing poems,
I talk about the indifference of nature.

It was soon after my mother died,
a brilliant June day,
everything blooming.

I sat on a gray stone bench
in a lovingly planted garden,
but the daylilies were as deaf
as the ears of drunken sleepers
and the roses curved inward.
Nothing was black or broken
and not a leaf fell
and the sun blared endless commercials
for summer holidays.

I sat on a gray stone bench
ringed with the ingénue faces
of pink and white impatiens
and placed my grief
in the mouth of language,
the only thing that would grieve with me.

Like Water on the Brain

Matthew Jacob Nadelson

> *for my grandfather, Eugene Hallan, 1921-2006*

I was standing in the garden
when a drop of rain fell upon the back
of my neck, and a shiver shot down my spine.

And isn't that the way our memories work?
Something jogs the senses—a smell
or the ache for the familiar

touch of a loved one and the memory
of some event seems to fall from nowhere
into the wellsprings of the mind the way

the earthy scent of these geranium
blossoms bowing down to drink
from this dark pool forming in the mud,

which seem hardly blossoms at all,
but the essence of green itself,
reminds me of a childhood trip

to Seattle to see my grandfather,
along whose home geraniums
grew in profusion, before Dementia

began to restrict the blood flow
to the realm of memory in his brain,
and oxygen tubes wormed their way

to his leaf-veined lungs the way this fallen
blossom has withered and gone gray
as a mind washed clean by darkness.

I Will Come Back

Pablo Neruda
   Translated by Alastair Reid

Some time, man or woman, traveller,
afterwards, when I am not alive,
look here, look for me here
between the stones and the ocean,
in the light storming
in the foam.
Look here, look for me here,
for here is where I shall come, saying nothing,
no voice, no mouth, pure,
here I shall be again the movement
of the water, of
its wild heart,
here I shall be both lost and found—
here I shall be perhaps both stone and silence.

ODE TO SOME YELLOW FLOWERS

Pablo Neruda
   Translated by Mara and Ray Smith

Against the blue shifting its blues
the sea, and against the sky
some yellow flowers.

October comes.

And although it may seem
so important, the sea unrolling
its myth, its mission, its turgor,
there bursts
over the sand the gold
of a single
yellow plant
and your eyes
rivet themselves
to the earth.
They avoid the great sea and its throbbing.

   Earth we are, we shall be
   not air, not fire, not water

but
earth,
only earth,
we shall be
and, perhaps,
some yellow flowers.

My Grandmother in the Stars

Naomi Shihab Nye

It is possible we will not meet again
on earth. To think this fills my throat
with dust. Then there is only the sky
tying the universe together.

Just now the neighbor's horse must be standing
patiently, hoof on stone, waiting for his day
to open. What you think of him,
and the village's one heroic cow,
is the knowledge I wish to gather.
I bow to your rugged feet,
the moth-eaten scarves that knot your hair.

Where we live in the world
is never one place. Our hearts,
those dogged mirrors, keep flashing us
moons before we are ready for them.
You and I on a roof at sunset,
our two languages adrift,
heart saying, Take this home with you,
never again,
and only memory making us rich.

Preparing for Grief

Patricia O'Donnell

Buy the snazzy suit, don't skimp;
dark, solid, and—get this—rock hard.
Bullets and missiles would ricochet.
Keep it cleaned and pressed.
Change the oil in your car, and buy new tires.
It won't be you, this time,
broken-down by the side of the road
in the pouring rain, on your way
to the impossible important place.
It won't be you.

Find a hairstyle that flatters, yet is easy.
On the awful morning you won't have time to fuss,
to curl or polish. It won't be you whose hair hangs,
unbrushed, ungainly and sad,
when grief-seekers
sneak a glance.

There are many things I could tell you,
but I doubt if you'll listen.
Collect phrases,
all of them the right one,
to strew like broken flowers across parking lots.
Perfect a face which draws only brief glances.
Hold nothing too long, and shy away
from being held. Watch old movies to learn
the cool yet natural eyes, the mouth
whose kiss is a defense.

And this is especially crucial:
Forget the past. All of it, all its fragrant corners,
all its blossomy mornings. It did not
exist. It did not,
and so can not come sweeping from behind as
you walk down some hall, catching the back of your
knees unaware, buckling you
in the excess of all you'd planned
to avoid.

CLOSE TO DEATH

Sharon Olds

Always, now, I feel it, a steady
even pressure, all over my body,
as if I were held in a flower-press.
I am waiting for the phone to ring,
they will say it and I will not be ready,
I do not have a place prepared,
I do not know what will happen to him
or where he will go. I always thought
I had a salvation for him, hidden,
even from myself, in my chest. But when the phone rings,
I don't know who he will be, then,
or where, I have nothing for him, no net,
no heaven to catch him—he taught me only
the earth, night, sleep, the male
body in its beauty and fearsomeness,
he set up that landscape for me
to go to him in, and I will go to him
and give to him, what he gave me I will give him,
the earth, night, sleep, beauty, fear.

WHEN DEATH COMES

Mary Oliver

When death comes
like the hungry bear in autumn;
when death comes and takes all the bright coins from his purse

to buy me, and snaps the purse shut;
when death comes
like the measle-pox;

when death comes
like an iceberg between the shoulder blades,

I want to step through the door full of curiosity, wondering:
what is it going to be like, that cottage of darkness?

And therefore I look upon everything
as a brotherhood and a sisterhood,
and I look upon time as no more than an idea,
and I consider eternity as another possibility,

and I think of each life as a flower, as common
as a field daisy, and as singular,

and each name a comfortable music in the mouth,
tending, as all music does, toward silence,

and each body a lion of courage, and something
precious to the earth.

When it's over, I want to say: all my life
I was a bride married to amazement.
I was the bridegroom, taking the world into my arms.

When it's over, I don't want to wonder
if I have made of my life something particular, and real.
I don't want to find myself sighing and frightened,
or full of argument.

I don't want to end up simply having visited this world.

In Blackwater Woods

Mary Oliver

Look, the trees
are turning
their own bodies
into pillars

of light,
are giving off the rich
fragrance of cinnamon
and fulfillment.

The long tapers
of cattails
are bursting and floating away over
the blue shoulders
of the ponds,
and every pond
no matter what its
name is, is

nameless now.
Every year
everything
I have ever learned

in my lifetime
leads back to this: the fires
and the black river of loss
whose other side

is salvation,
whose meaning
none of us will ever know.
To live in this world

you must be able
to do three things:
to love what is mortal,
to hold it

against your bones knowing
your own life depends on it;
and, when the time comes to let it go,
to let it go.

MIGRATIONS: DULUTH, MINNESOTA

Sheila Packa

read hawk's story   ink scrawls
across   a paper sky   the good-bye
to time
a woman turning through wrinkled
leaves
the wood is in   the garden
is in   the wash
the wind wraps all of us
with winter
almost silence
then melts ice into spring
tongues loosen
she snaps twigs
beneath her tie-shoes
on the unpaved road
in her coat is a tomato
from the window sill
the choker chain from the dog
in her coat is all the wilderness
from here to the border
beating like the heart of a hare
under   the shadow

she is my grandmother
coming to get me
her children are the
wild life
asleep in the woods

until my grandfather returns
to the lumber camp
a dump of rusted cans and broken bottles
in his swath
no money   fear
another conception
she midwifed herself
made do by selling eggs

the past is north
the past is the fledgling
inside the fall
hawk migration
my grandmother married at sixteen
she told me
don't
my grandmother had eleven kids
she said
too many tie you down

she broke the tether of her body
at the age of eighty two
in the virgin forest
where I've come to live

now   the sky
wakes to the kettling hawks
I wake to her
to all the emigrants   fierce
wings
over the flame
of leaves

DANS MACABRE

Nancy Paddock

All night the snow fell, muting harsh outlines,
clinging to each twig, each branch,
a tracery of white against the blank sky,
white as the fine dust of calcium,
your bodies now,
my mother, my father.

To crying flutes,
shouts and yips,
the heartbeat of Inca drums,
I am dancing your deaths.

I spin, arms raised in praise of you,
in praise of earth
and your blood that beats
in my breaking heart.

I dance
the *dans macabre* that is life
when the soul opens without fear

allowing the sorrow,

allowing the joy
that will die.

The Death of a Parent

Linda Pastan

Move to the front
of the line
a voice says, and suddenly
there is nobody
left standing between you
and the world, to take
the first blows
on their shoulders.
This is the place in books
where part one ends, and
part two begins,
and there is no part three.
The slate is wiped
not clean but like a canvas
painted over in white
so that a whole new landscape
must be started,
bits of the old
still showing underneath—
those colors sadness lends
to a certain hour of evening.
Now the line of light
at the horizon
is the hinge between earth
and heaven, only visible
a few moments
as the sun drops
its rusted padlock
into place.

GO GENTLE

Linda Pastan

You have grown wings of pain
and flap around the bed like a wounded gull
calling for water, calling for tea, for grapes
whose skin you cannot penetrate.
Remember when you taught me
how to swim? Let go, you said,
the lake will hold you up.
I long to say, Father let go
and death will hold you up.
Outside the fall goes on without us.
How easily the leaves give in,
I hear them on the last breath of wind,
passing this disappearing place.

HOW TO SAVE THE DAY

Roger Pfingston

   for D.T.

How to save the day
since you cannot save
your father: wake,
touch the naked silk
of your wife, rise to see
how your children sleep;
be alone in the first light,
alive in a room as simple
as air: eat, drink…call
your friends by name
until you sing again
in a poem of your own,
addressing the day, at last,
as if it were your father.

WHY I WEAR MY HAIR LONG

Marge Piercy

My mother always wore her hair cropped;
mine she braided tight into rubberbands.
The mistrust of hair was general then.

My grandmother had hair like Rapunzel
that she let down cascading before
she climbed into bed with me.

Loosely braided around her head all
day, at night it tumbled free, giving
off an odor of lavender and something

else, almost musky, signifying at
eighty and blind, she was still
a woman. She taught me Hebrew

prayers, she taught me Lilith,
the golem, dybbuks and flying rabbis,
raping, murderous Cossacks,

blood in the stetl, curses, escapes.
History and legend were braided
Into one thick musky rope that led

me back where she was born, back
into ghosts and demons and fierce
flaming angels and love, laps of love.

MAKING YOU LIVE IN THIS WAY

Andrea Potos

for my grandfather, on the fourth anniversary of his death.

This year, I don't light the chapel candle
I usually set before your photograph.

I quench my blaze of temper
when my daughter's will springs to block mine.

I kneel beside her
to cut out clouds from blue

and purple construction paper.
I thank my husband for his morning impulse

of fresh bagels.
I hold his warm hands,

forget to look at the clock.
Calmness spreads like a meadow within me.

As the hours unfold, I repeat often
the one word you were known for:

beautiful, beautiful.

ALLOWING GRACE

Judith E. Prest

I am dancing
balanced on the edge
between worlds,
memories telescoping
playing simultaneously
with dreams and reality
a festival of images

I accept death
inviting it as a beginning
I am watching my mother's illusions
collapse around her
piling high in the hospital bed
filling the space so she barely has room
I am watching her hang on,
hands clawed with arthritis,
frozen on the wheel of her life
grasping, seeking,
resisting…

I sing lullabies in my head
I float above the room
out the window, between bare branches
follow the river of migrating blackbirds,
rise with the moon
dance with the wind

Somewhere the child I was is wailing
I grieve the loss of mother

accept that for now I am mothering her
and myself as well

I hold her hands
feel the bones so near the surface
sense her spirit not yet unbound
release my claim on her being
releasing with love
enduring, dreaming, dancing with spirit

I imagine heartbeats: hers fainter, mine steady
all centered, aligned with the universe
praying for patience, praying for endurance
praying for the gift of
allowing grace.

PUEBLO BLESSING

Hold onto what is good
Even if it is a handful of earth.

Hold onto what you believe
Even if it is a tree that stands by itself.

Hold onto what you must do
Even if it is a long way from here.

Hold onto life
Even if it seems easier to let go.

Hold onto my hand
Even if I have gone away from you.

"THIS PLACE OF SKULL WHERE I HEAR MYSELF WEEPING"

—James Wright, *Listening to the mourners*

Carlos Reyes

for Sara who remains among us

Though you hide
way back in my skull
cupping in small hands
an ebony box labeled
in careful calligraphy,

I cradle you in my arms
after all these years
each time I hold a baby.

As I perform that simple
act, the black box fades

until I put *you* down
then a child's voice
walks back to me
through the fog calling
father

until you are
your own mother
raging at me *where are you?*

I am here, your father
drunk
with loneliness

sadness and remorse.

The grief I have
is your life somewhere
I remember and
calculate your age
how old you would be
trying to imagine
what you'd look like.

As I set my grandchild down
the black box returns.

I remove it
from the room of my skull,
send it out on
black waters
of the other world
with this note.

If you find it drifted
onto some river bank,
amongst the willow reeds
or at the base
of some great ash,

ease my years
the guilt
I could not confess,

take it for what
it means, *forgive me.*

TATTERED KADDISH

Adrienne Rich

Taurean reaper of the wild apple field
messenger from the earthmire gleaning
transcripts of fog
in the nineteenth year and eleventh month
speak your tattered Kaddish for all suicides:

Praise to life though it crumbled in like a tunnel
on ones we knew and loved

>Praise to life though its windows blew shut
>on the breathing-room of ones we knew and loved

Praise to life though ones we knew and loved
loved it badly, too well, and not enough

>Praise to life though it tightened like a knot
>on the hearts of ones we thought we knew loved us

Praise to life giving room and reason
to ones we knew and loved who felt unpraisable

>Praise to them, how they loved it, when they could.

MUTED GOLD

Susan Rich

for Abraham Rich

My father died just as my plane touched down.
He taught me journeys don't happen in straight lines.
I loved him without ever needing words.
Is memory a chain of alibis?

He taught me journeys don't happen in straight lines.
His father sailed Odessa to Boston Harbor.
Is memory a chain of alibis?
The story I choose a net of my own desires?

His father sailed Odessa to Boston Harbor.
Dad worked beside him in their corner store.
The story I choose a net of my own desires?
I wish I'd known to ask the simple questions.

Dad worked beside him in their corner store.
They shelved the tins of black beans, fruit preserves, and almond cakes.
I wish I'd known to ask the simple questions,
he'd have stayed with me and gossiped over toast.

They shelved the tins of black beans, fruit preserves and almond cakes.
What colors did they wear, what languages were spoken?
He'd have stayed with me and gossiped over toast,
now he's smiling but I can't summon the thoughts he's thinking.

What colors did they wear, what languages were spoken?
Was it a muted gold, a world of shattered feeling?
Now he's smiling but I can't summon the thoughts he's thinking.

I pack his clothes away, mark them *for Goodwill.*

Was it a muted gold, a world of shattered feeling?
What good will it do to dwell, I hear him say.
I pack his clothes away, mark them *for Goodwill.*
but I hold fast to one old T shirt, butter-smooth, and brilliant.

What good will it do to dwell, I hear him say.
He much preferred to glide along life's surface.
But I hold fast to one old T shirt, butter-smooth, and brilliant
and tell a story by moonlight, to try and keep him with me.

He much preferred to glide along life's surface.
I love him now with images and words,
and tell a story by moonlight, to try and keep him with me.
My father died just as my plane touched down.

THE SWAN

Rainer Maria Rilke
Translator unknown

This clumsy living,
that moves lumbering
as if in ropes
through what is not done,
reminds us of the awkward way
the swan walks.

And to die,
which is a letting go
of the ground we stand on
and cling to every day,
is like the swan
when he nervously
lets himself down
into the water,

which receives him gaily
and which flows joyfully
under him and after him,
wave after wave,
while the swan, unmoving
and marvelously calm,
is pleased to be carried,

each moment more fully grown,
more like a king, composed,
farther and farther on.

Sitting With Grandma

Gail Rixen

Something always makes you look up
when I come: the skin, the shape.
I have not had a name for years.
Hands now fold over your belly,
quiet, without a project.
Hands that made every grandchild
the softest flannel gown,
that always browned the onions
with the burger,
that bedded petunias in the old minnow tank.
Every little doing a joy.

You were Christmas, hotdish, and Liberace,
Lillian Gish and Ma Kettle
till the piano, stove, and memory failed you.
Your handwriting in the newspaper margins
making the copied words beautiful
before they went away.
For everything you stitched up neat,
Kinde, tusen takk.

I am sitting here now as you doze,
not in case you remember me,
but because I remember you.

I Weave Memories

George Roberts

I weave memories of the dead — mother,
father, sister — into a circle and stand inside.

Their hands reach up from the darkness.
Their voices say my name like old photographs.

They stand on the shoulders of others who have shed
their names, shed their labels of mother, father, sister...

Nameless then, without stories, a wreath
of flowers coming apart on moving water.

Without stories memory blurs like a child's
drawing on the sidewalk in the rain.

Stories teach us to accept the fading
of photographs, and flowers.

We sink into the watery darkness, reaching
our hands up, as if to say goodbye.

FULL MOON OVER THE ALLEGHENY

Helen Ruggieri

one month
since you followed
the moon road
over dark water

one month
since the moon
waned taking you
with her

full circle of light
dropped behind the hills
burned away
only the ashes

gray on dark water
for a moment
eddy into the current
where moonlight crosses

AUTUMN ROSE ELEGY

Rumi
Translated by Coleman Barks

You have gone to the secret world.
Which way is it?
You broke the cage and flew.
You heard the drum that calls you home.

You left this humiliating shelf,
this disorienting desert,
where we are given wrong direction.

What use now a crown?
You have become the sun.
No need for a belt.
You have slipped out of your waist.

I have heard that near the end
you were eyes looking at soul.
No more looking now.
You live inside the soul.

You are the strange autumn rose
that led the winter wind in by withering.

You are rain soaking everywhere from cloud to ground.
No bother of talking.
Flowing silence and sweet sleep beside the friend.

THINGS SHOULDN'T BE SO HARD

Kay Ryan

A life should leave
deep tracks:
ruts where she
went out and back
to get the mail
or move the hose
around the yard;
where she used to
stand before the sink,
a worn-out place;
beneath her hand
the china knobs
rubbed down to
white pastilles;
the switch she
used to feel for
in the dark
almost erased.
Her things should
keep her marks.
The passage
of a life
should show;
it should abrade.
And when life stops,
a certain space—
however small—
should be left scarred

by the grand and
damaging parade.
Things shouldn't
be so hard.

PSYCH WARD

Edith Rylander

   for my mother

Now as I talk to these people, sign these papers,
I remember I was one of the world's great cryers.
I sit here calm-faced, watching the sun glare
Off a drab-painted wall.
                       Where are the tears
I gave to Keats, and the Joads, and my Dad's harmony,
And Frodo Baggins, and little kids in commercials?
She clings and clings to me, who is as far from me
In the orbit of her mind as those strange stars
Which fall in on themselves and give no light,
Their gravity being beyond what we even dream;
We easy cryers, we cheerful junkies of hope.
I will walk off down that hall past those doors and that bright
Poster for exercise class. I will not scream.
If I start crying now, I will never stop.

MUSAF: ADDITIONAL PRAYER

Kenneth Salzmann

Praised be the one
I have lived contentedly without;
who reveals the Berkshires today
are an unexpected house of prayer
and sorrow, as just one green month
rises to repair a broken circle; whose
search for me is unfulfilled
and perhaps not ended.

Blessed is eternal loss and glory, wonder of the universe,
splash of color slipping from a winter-weary wood
that I have often walked alone; blessed a father's flight
that leaves a son with no direction to flee but back
along remembered village roads that run two ways
through dimming childhoods; blessed each step out
and each step back, the returning implicit in the going.

Blessed are the little-traveled village roads that carry
fathers and sons toward innumerable destinations.

Blessed are the four corners, and the fringes.

Eternal Mothering Presence, you coax *Deuteronomy*
from the gentle throats of Berkshire songbirds
and fly away; you clothe the naked birches
with the finishing touches of spring; you drop green vowels
on weathered wood until the world finds a voice
and whispers *Shema*; you make me a Jew.

Unending *Adonai*, help us to go on imagining
that, wherever we go, we have only missed you
by a moment; allow us our untenable conviction
that we might become a blessing.

Blessed Father, command us to be free.

Sonnet 2 from "The Autumn Sonnets"

May Sarton

If I can let you go as trees let go
Their leaves, so casually, one by one;
If I can come to know what they do know,
That fall is the release, the consummation,
Then fear of time and the uncertain fruit
Would not distemper the great lucid skies
This strangest autumn, mellow and acute.
If I can take the dark with open eyes
And call it seasonal, not harsh or strange
(For love itself may need a time of sleep),
And, treelike, stand unmoved before the change,
Lose what I lose to keep what I can keep,
The strong root still alive under the snow,
Love will endure—if I can let you go.

BEARING

Larry Schug

She bore six sons,
One for each handle
Of her coffin;
Three left hands,
Three right,
Never clung so tight
To anything.

MADRIGAL

Noelle Sickels

> *for Brent*

Let's repeat the song of
summer gutters rushing rainwater
asphalt still warm under bare feet
its wet scent sharp in our nostrils
my brother filling his pockets with worms
flooded out of earthen homes

Let's repeat the song of
woolen Army blanket spread on crabgrass
itchy at the backs of our skinny knees
grape juice in tall metal tumblers
the taste of iced aluminum
making the back of my mouth water
as if it were crying

Let's repeat the song of
rotten apples in the autumn yard
circling, avaricious yellow jackets
raking was supposed to be my brother's job
while we girls set table, sorted laundry
rocked the eternal baby
but there were too many apples for one boy alone
he was so sluggish we were dispatched to help

Let's repeat the song of
eave icicles carefully broken off
fast-melting spikes tasting mildly of dirt

snow-packed ice-slick Terhune Street
hard trudge up, dizzying flight down
my brother's last minute veer
from River Road slush and traffic
into drifts built by plows while we slept

Let's repeat the song of
breaking glass and blood, later regrets and stitches
when I locked my brother outside in his underwear
he pounded the door and I couldn't let him in
too afraid of his desperate outrage
the angry squall in his dark eyes

Let's repeat the song of
plays we put on for our parents
I was always director and sometimes actor, too
melodramas about orphans
that managed to feature a romance
obligating my brother to kiss a sister on the mouth
but only after both had held their breath
and folded their lips in tight over teeth

Let's repeat the song of
board games and card games
heated disputes and do-overs
whether the Pick-Up stick moved
which number the spinner stopped on
my brother played with ardor
believed he could make luck
fanned out his paper money, rubbed the dice
would not let me quit Monopoly, concede at checkers
insisting I count on chance, not give up hope

Let's repeat the song of
men moving through the neighborhood
scissors man hunched in his oily truck

gray grindstone sparking knives, mower blades
Fuller Brush man on housebound afternoons
wide case of brushes, combs, creams, brooms
early morning bounty of Dugan Bread man
we took turns picking treats from his big basket
Good Humor man on summer nights
white shirt, white pants, trim white mustache
I always got a toasted almond bar
my brother chose differently every time

Let's repeat the last song, too
my brother at 50, magician, gambler
cancer coarsening his slow voice
scorned doctors, banked on other healers
potions, purges, light machine
he would not say good-bye
all his families slipknots on a silken cord

Let us repeat, repeat
our final day together
his lanky, ravished body regal still
stretched out on living room floor
watching the Oscars
he yearned, in the end, for simple things
to work up a sweat in the garden
to drive through the desert, top down
to play poker and win

BLACK AND WHITE PHOTOGRAPH

James Siegel

Sun patches slipped
along your curls
in mid-October.
You were fifteen

feet ahead of me.
We walked
below the leaves—
green with a shadow

breath of yellow
and the brown ones
scattered on the red
needled floor crunched

underfoot so I, a child,
left lurching footprints,
pitching myself
on leaf branches.

~

Today the faint line
of your mastectomy
stretches over a pouch

of saline. Your
desire stronger
than your balance

you wrap your
head in gypsy
cloth. I drive us

down Bradford Street
where rain slacks
off the tires & question

marks hunch
across pavement
under umbrellas

~

The tide readies to ebb
Does rain bend the familiar

streets fold the old
storefronts distort

the breakwater
down the windshield

I am a bug in amber
The docks and moorings

rap winter the lighthouse
writhes against the sky

~

You plucked tufts of hair.

Tired wisps clung to your crown.

The color beneath our footprints

Is buried under glass.

THROUGH THE WOODS

Anne Simpson

Walking through dark woods
we drop memories
like bread crumbs,
as if they could lead us back
to a past devoured.

We hold what we can
of love and grief,
slowly weave our way toward the clearing
where they will become one.

We rest to take deep gulps
of sweet pungent air;
we share the bread left over.

AFTERLIFE

Floyd Skloot

He said he believed in life after death.
The proof would be his haunting the landscape
here. I would see him in the shifting breath
of wind when a storm blew in from the cape,
the flash of bittersweet light at dawn,
the time he loved best, or in a wren's song.
I would see and hear my brother's own
life linger in mine, and look for him in long
drawn-out moments before the tide turns,
or in winter rains that never seem to end.
There he is, in the drenched sword fern's
steady drip after the skies clear, in the bend
of its leaves, the deeper greening. Or now,
in sun laced by haze, the way flaring beams
pinpoint moss on a newly fallen oak bough
instead of the solid earth on which it leans.

REMNANTS

Emily Louise Smith

Everything slipped into the vacuum
that was my grandmother
in those years. Footsteps, voices
from the muted television set.
We tiptoed in her house, tried not to let Dad
catch us staring at her legless nubs.

Gradually, her body was receding.
We didn't understand that we were watching
her die. We'd been to Sunday school enough
to form a theory: if she wouldn't go
gracefully, God would take her
a section at a time. First, one leg. Then
the second. Then her hair from its tidy knot.

Once at home in high-ceilinged rooms, the order
of wainscoting and mantels, she now retired
to the first floor den turned bedroom.
Granddad lifted her from wheelchair to bed.
The house so still, she must have heard the wake
of ball gowns, banter on the veranda, felt
herself floating among the guests.

Her gloved fingers knew light switches
and balustrades, even in the dark, how to negotiate
settees, curios, and end tables. Once we
moved in, it would take years to traverse
rooms without tripping, memorize the map
back to my grandfather.

Amid the clutter of an upstairs room, I find
a box of letters, the flimsy page where
a former admirer scribbled, *your presence
lit up the room*. Farther down, he describes time
spent without her as overwhelming. Touching

that word now, I think so much better, his
insatiable emptiness. That kind goes away.
Try living with her whittled down to her parts.
On the back of a photograph, in the bottom
of a chest, she shed pieces of herself. Even lifting her
handkerchief more than a decade after
she died, I uncover a new perfume of grief.

ELEGY

Joseph A. Soldati

On my father's gravestone, only his name,
his life bracketed by the years he lived.
My mother's—not even her name, just
her initials, as she requested. No *Beloved*
this or *that*; no bas-relief of *Requiescat*
in pace, no marble angels airing
their wings, or carved cherubs blaring
cornets. My parents' ashes lie boxed
and buried beneath oaks in both Carolinas,
such was and is their separation.

In the empty chambers among the trees
mockingbirds and cardinals distill the air
into Southern song. Even in summer—
the air so hot and thick it seems borrowed
from a laundry, and you think a breeze
will never come—a chord from one bird
or another wafts cool, heart-piercing,
a lovely lonely song, like one you could hear
years ago humming from a shanty
or strummed from a cabin in the Blue Ridge.

Song that resonates their loss and mine
as I stand before my mother's grave,
mindful of the miles that separate this site
from the other. Sad parting song under
the canopy of old trees, the descending
night and the phosphorescence of rising
fireflies. Attending song for the miles

I must travel in the dark, harsh highway
and insects in the headlights, the radio silent,
to reach my father's grave by morning.

GRIEF COMES WITH A LADDER

Richard Solly

> *for Kay*

Friend, you ask when it will end.
All I know is that grief comes with a ladder,

though not for ascending. Try to decipher
the language of leaves, other faces, as strange

as they appear. Its alphabet will not make sense.
Nothing, not even birds, exists now as they should.

Never mind them. Their songs belong elsewhere.
Your task is clear. Climb, one hand, one foot,

one after another takes you there. You ask:
Do words help? Remember. The truest prayer

is said before you utter its words. Like the wind
stirs the feathers of a still bird. The words

themselves that lift into the air don't matter,
only the silence and sky that summon you.

I know only this: as you reach the last rung,
as your clothes become threadbare, as hope

becomes a whisper, a reversal happens.
Like water, when it's displaced by a weight,

rises, and is now overflowing the brim.
What took you down now takes you up.

One morning, a sign of change:
shade under the leaves of a small tree.

FOR A LOST CHILD

William Stafford

What happens is, the kind of snow that sweeps
Wyoming comes down while I'm asleep. Dawn
finds our sleeping bag but you are gone.
Nowhere now, you call through every storm,
a voice that wanders without a home.

Across bridges that used to find a shore
you pass, and along shadows of trees that fell
before you were born. You are a memory
too strong to leave this world that slips away
even as its precious time goes on.

I glimpse you often, faithful to every country
we ever found, a bright shadow the sun
forgot one day. On a map of Spain
I find your note left from a trip that year
our family traveled: "Daddy, we could meet here."

ORIGAMI

Barry Sternlieb

For the last time
hold our children close.
First the older, who will slowly
forget you, and then the baby
who touches your delicate mouth,
each smooth eyefold, and that fragrant
sleep-colored hair.

You must have felt the journey
come to life before we understood
what was happening, an October-like
change in countenance, a pond
abandoned.

But the peaks of your voice
are crystalline with new growth,
acceptance channeling sun into pulse
as our daughters give way
just enough to watch your hands spawn
a swan from paper, deftly,
arced neck and impossible
wings appear.

Inside minutes, complete,
it's set on the mantel
between bronze stag and earthen ram;
suddenly faced
with your leaving,
we cannot fathom the intricacy

of so controlled a flight, your mind
performing as if nourished by loss
for a thousand fragile years.

BALANCE OF POWER

Barry Sternlieb

It does me good
to watch cold come to light
in these hills
because I'm through
splitting a winter
of birch and maple,
and pipe lit, collar up,
feel the burning
heart in horizon
stop long enough to recall
tomorrow you will be gone
ten years. Geese will wave
past the house, and old hornets,
drunk on sun, will stagger
from clothesline to porchrail.
The urge to fly has brought me
the happiness of knowing
I can't. Look down that road:
Wind relays the quiet
belief in life
lasting another day.

AFTER THE FUNERAL

Anne Stewart

Headlights track the highway
across the night-smothered snow.
The incessant susurration of tires moves us
through a galaxy of farms, towns,
radio tower lights pulsing like super nova,
riding me back in memory—
traveling homeward half asleep
in mother's lap, stroking
the fur collar of her coat.

We turn into the driveway.
The porch light is on. Our child,
innocent of time, stands at the door.
I pick him up, carry him up the stairs,
sit down in Mother's rocker by the window,
absorb the measure of the small body against mine,
fit us into space gone barren.

Outside, cars on our road meet,
dim lights,
move on.

My Mother's Room

Myrna Stone

Begin to look for the dead and you'll find them,
here and here and here, in the window's strict

rectangular divisions of what light, in this early-
gathering dusk, remains, and in the yard beyond,

its ornamental fall, adrift now in smoke, in a last
turning of the year, and here, in this ivory-backed

brush and comb joined on the bureau, in ropes
of pearls that still spill from their box a radiant

disorder, in a scent so distinct, so dense
with orchids, you must dab it once, and only once

behind your ears—and finally here, in this precisely-
folded quilted robe stored in the bureau's bottom drawer.

How suddenly she is home for the last time again,
bound by this red cloth, by sleep, to the bed, her hands

angular against her breast, cupped one over the other
over an absence. Nothing will happen for hours . . . .

If there is power in the union of memory and desire
it is manifest in this place, this diminishing light,

each enduring object of her bodily life its witness
so that even now she has risen to stand by the window,

to welcome this transforming moment, this whole
overcast season given over, as it was then, to earth.

Words for My Mother

Myrna Stone

(1)

And when we each had been summoned
and gathered, flesh of your flesh,
   at your bedside in that last stark, antiseptic

  room, we found in your absence no new
language of argument or touch to wrest
   or rouse you. Detained in the heavy traffic

  of transit, unmoored from this world
and not yet delivered to another,
   you couldn't know the import we assigned

  every detail of your passage: September,
the eleventh day and its eleventh hour,
   how the shuttered light from the window

  began to build, to put down on your face
its first thin, yellow planks of morning,
   or how, in the final moment of your transport,

  we longed for what you, too, must have
longed for: some sign, some portent
   of perpetuation, and how to believe it.

(2)

If I could bring you back again
  it would be on a day like this when rain

has washed and washed the air, and wind
        is a sort of speech the sky transmits between

each black and barren bough.
        And I would bring you in and tell you this
is what I love: this landscape, these rooms
        you've never seen, the slow seamless hours

of the afternoon unfolding
        like weather, disclosing all their vacancies
and varied plenties. And I would offer you
        tea in a painted china cup, and cake on a silver

plate, and serve it on linen
        from my best gateleg table opened before
the fire. Here, I would say, is my life
        and these are the words I've written for you.

And if you began to speak to me
        of what desire is like on the opposing
plane, of what extreme punishments
        or pleasures await even the least of us

I would dissuade you,
        I would kiss your cheek and lead you here
to this room, to this chair, this desk
        and this window's suddenly luminescent view.

OCTOBER, FIRST SNOW

Thom Tammaro

for my father

Late afternoon. When it arrives,
I am not ready for it.

This white reminding me of
the time I noticed your first gray hair
dusting your temples
and thought of apple blossoms.

And near the end, when ashes fell
from your cigarette onto the white sheets
and I pretended not to notice
then brushed them away.

Almost six months since your departure.
How you will not let go.

But this gray afternoon
temporarily lifted by this whiteness—
a momentary reprieve from grief—
born again and again into
the harshness of this season.

The green grass turning white,
the dark windshields of parked cars brightening.

MYTH

Natasha Trethewey

I was asleep while you were dying.
It's as if you slipped through some rift, a hollow
I make between my slumber and my waking,

the Erebus I keep you in, still trying
not to let go. You'll be dead again tomorrow,
but in dreams you live. So I try taking

you back into morning. Sleep-heavy, turning,
my eyes open, I find you do not follow.
Again and again, this constant forsaking.

~

Again and again, this constant forsaking:
my eyes open, I find you do not follow.
You back into morning, sleep-heavy, turning.

But in dreams you live. So I try taking,
not to let go. You'll be dead again tomorrow.
The Erebus I keep you in—still, trying—

I make between my slumber and my waking.
It's as if you slipped through some rift, a hollow.
I was asleep while you were dying.

After Your Death

Natasha Trethewey

First, I emptied the closets of your clothes,
threw out the bowl of fruit, bruised
from your touch, left empty the jars

you bought for preserves. The next morning,
birds rustled the fruit trees, and later
when I twisted a ripe fig loose from its stem,

I found it half eaten, the other side
already rotting, or—like another I plucked
and split open—being taken from the inside:

a swarm of insects hollowing it. I'm too late,
again, another space emptied by loss.
Tomorrow, the bowl I have yet to fill.

THE WIZARD OF DIRT

Claudia Van Gerven

I would watch you long summer Saturdays
from my bedroom window. You had hung
your accountant's suit in the closet, rolled up

your sleeves, donned sweat-stained fedora
to transubstantiate from distant, taciturn father
into a sorcerer wheeling barrows full of precious loam,

through afternoon shadows, fingers itching to call forth
fierce spirits of dahlias, hyacinth. Summers you walked
through rows of ripening corn till pollen clung

to the brim of your hat, the backs of your hands,
gold leaf on a young god. You were in your glory,
an unearthly earthiness. You fingered dirt

weighed it in the palm of your hand,
cupped it to your ear as if listening
to some lost inland sea, sniffed it the way

a man smells a woman's slip just fallen
to the floor. You knew just from its scent
what it wanted: more compost, a touch of nitrogen.

You were never stingy with soil.

You showed me one off hand summer how to taste
dirt, to know its essence from the tang. I took
a pinch between thumb and forefinger

relished the mineral zest, the pungent aftertaste.
Death, you said, gave dirt its flavor.

Now a decade after your death I wonder
if you are happy in your bland Mormon heaven,
every one singing hymns in white robes, the earth

redeemed of death, or do you mingle with your first true
love, lapped in that decadent loam. Is it your contradictions
I taste in the slippery meat of my beefsteak tomatoes,

Does your life, your death, flavor my wind-
fallen Jonathans, bruised sides tonguing earth's savor?

DEAD BROTHERS

Claudia Van Gerven

My friend imagines her brother at a bookstore café
surrounded in good humor and pastry crumbs.
She wants him to see the easy grace
of his grown son, how the world spins out
its webs of words in fiber optics. She wants to
give him books on sex and feed him
cornbread and baked potatoes, white and solid
beneath brown blistered skins.

I try to think what I would give
my brother, what he gave to me.
I remember only one thing:

a June morning liquid
with new leaves, new sky.
I am perched on the handlebars
of his old green Schwinn. Little shadows
flitter around us like nervous songs.
I look down at my white anklets
my own small legs dangling
from my new blue dress. I am going

to kindergarten. I am all grown up
and he has been conscripted to take me.
I do not see his freckled face, his brushcut
the gap toothed smile I suspect
he was not smiling. I can't turn around,
but only look forward to the chain
link fences of Sherman Elementary approaching

with its alphabets, and building blocks.

We do not speak. I only know he's there
because I feel the sway of the bicycle
as he pumps, how he stands up
sometimes to thrust us forward.
And perhaps I hear his breath
catching, laboring as he struggles to deliver me
to a new world.

But Jane, I Have Seen the Room Weep

Sherre Vernon

> *A room does not turn its back on grief.*
> *Anger does not excite it.*
> —from Jane Hirshfield's "A Room"

Each aspect shifts: the table melds itself
to an altar; an old cloth
reknots its lace to a murmuring shroud.
Even the chairs show fear—

in grief, they cringe, sink, begin
to molt
unused paint;
they falter, flit, on loose-turned legs.

There is no staid welcoming
of death's stillness.
Even the wallpipes wail a lean cacophony.

The doors, these are the most lost—
they refuse their latches, their mourning
a function of isolated wood, grains
abandoned and hinges rusted shut with anger.

The origin of this agony is not
at question here:

for a man whose eyes each morning took in
the smallest offertory of color—

absence matters. It measures
itself in corners and windowsills.
Asking is what is useless.

MEMORY CARE UNIT

Mark Vinz

"I don't know where I'm supposed to be,"
she says, beginning her rosary of
wringing hands. If past is prologue,
then tomorrow is the day that never comes.

Myrtle simply babbles, fiercely
carpet sweeping clean wood floors
while Alma's off again to find
the sister she knows is waiting
somewhere just behind closed doors.
Jean's the cheerful one, proud to
remember piano tunes across the years
but not the face she talked to last.
"Where are you from?" she asks and
then replies "that's good" to every answer.

Enter here a world of women alone so long
they gather round each visitor, transfixed
by the flicker of something almost familiar,
as if whispers alone can hold them up.

"Where am I supposed to be?" she asks,
trusting me for any answer. I take her hand
and we recite those necessary names again:
mother, son, right here, right now, and *always.*

THIRD YAHRZEIT

Davi Walders

Perhaps, this May, I'll let the azaleas burst
into fuschia bloom, the dogwoods' leafy white
shimmer into green, and not hide, then run

from rivers raging forth like icy streams
breaking from their rocky beds. Perhaps this May
I'll see the stamen rise and curl like snails,

peaking from soft petaled pink, not crumpled
brown, withered, wet, like salted slugs that stained
my arm as I banged an almost orphaned knee to squeeze

between a metal crank and air-conditioner edge
that sprayed its drops on straws and gauze long
gone. Perhaps this May I will protect those knees,

these arms, other extremities—not zip into a blue-
curtained womb to let flat tracks, rods slashing pine,
flash me back towards home to cotton pods, refinery

smoke, bayous red and brown, nor fly a thousand
miles to walk a foreign path beneath grey Spanish
moss until sprinklers swished their spiral noose

on names and dying grass, nor let myself retrace
those steps, that loss back to a marble shining
slab to leave another smaller stone, as though

things once unveiled could be contained by pebbles,
weights. Perhaps this May no one will come to pray,
the house will lose its echoes, the scent of potted

plants, the musk of platters filled with pickled
fish, the foil, the bows, and words, each hackneyed
hatchet phrase, *"She was ready,"* *"God called her,"*

"Get a dog," *"Just stay busy."* Perhaps this spring
I'll simply mark the time, sit in a park beside
a lavender bush or in a kitchen newly painted pink,

a room without a wheelchair, pain, and let the shadows
play. Perhaps I'll hear a leaf brush the window screen,
say Kaddish as the wick begins to flame, or perhaps

this year I'll just pour a glass of wine, lift crystal
stem towards light, press lip against my lips and sip
in quiet peace before I whisper, *"l'Chayim."*

Among My Father's Belongings

Stephanie Walker

> *More to be desired are they than gold, yea, than much fine gold*
> —Psalms 19:10

We undertook the goliath task
of sorting through his possessions—
our father's life through his things—
parsing them out like rations of memory.

Here was every birthday card and crayoned letter,
mixed in among every kind of saw and shovel,
a wooden carving of a shepherd, and there,
in the dark corners of his desk,
his chemo pills and five smooth stones.

The pills he refused, as David had done
with Saul's gilded armor—their faith lay instead
in a hope for psalms and in those stones,
polished by the current of an Israeli brook.
We rolled them over in our hands.

That day, we left a little heavier,
stones in our pockets for our own raging giants.

I thought of those stones when old-testament hail fell,
grief-heavy and fist-sized,
on my late summer garden.

The winter vegetables, which I had hoped for
like the rain and patience that promised them, were gone.

I pulled their severed vines weeks later,
tugging, following them like a prophecy
across the path, into the shade of a sturdy bush
where I discovered five green and golden-red acorn squash,
smooth and cool—five rare and singular mercies.

DEPARTURE

Catherine Senne Wallace

Count backwards from one. Reconfigure
the loss. Lean into the fraction that seeks

to divide you. Take whatever pieces remain.
Wrap the warm arms of remembrance

around you. Want nothing more than the joy
of certain words. Bind them together with

nothing but all the time in the world. Then
perhaps you can tell me why absence

precedes the bird—why song takes flight before
clasped claws abandon the branch—why

the same song sung in a major key
comes back bent.

I still wonder where you went in winter—when
certain words huddled tooclosetogether—now

these middle-of-the-night white stars I talk to—these
paroxysms of exuberant light—may already be dead

—may have flung their souls into some black hole
in the southwest corner of the universe. I will

continue to sing to them
until their lights go out.

From *"*REQUIEM*"*

Jennifer Wallace

> *Do not mourn like those who have no hope.* —C.S. *Lewis*

Eternal Light

Where are they?
Those whose light made us more visible. . .

No one's footsteps. No merry whistle on the stairs.
The hand we reach for.

When we trudge back from the stony field
the world is strangely the same, except
for the rip on the couch where he sat,
a thinness on the curb where she played.
And the knocking of our dulled attention.

We draw a circle around where they were.
Faith flickers there.

Deliver Them

Yellowed by the sun,
the once-woeful field shines with time.
A north wind clips the tiny grasses
but we deny the season, keeping
the last azure in view. It wants to fly.

We know better than to tether what we love.
Our cup of shadow overflowing.

The blue azure whispers up
and merges with the sky.
Up ahead: the sun-drenched track, greed-free,
from which the wing departs
and the new blade emerges.

Teach us to unbolt the door.

Eternal Rest

We draw a circle around where they were.
Faith flickers there.

Perhaps we are here to free the sparks
from grief's too small box, to light the way
for You who planted death within us so deeply
for You who chafe against our dark.

We come from the unknown and return there believing —

The spinning earth, still as a deep lake.
The fallen tree whose log crumbles,
seed safely hidden in the clay.

—restless until we rest.

Perhaps we are here to make of earth a minor heaven
where birds will glide higher
in an air made more full
by the deads' barely audible sigh.

(These sections contain lines inspired by, borrowed from other poets/thinkers:
"Our cup of shadow overflowing" is from Antonio Machado's poem, "Siesta."
A "death planted in us so deeply" alludes to ideas contained in Rilke's *Book of Hours*. "Restless until we rest" is from St. Augustine.)

The Death of My Father

Connie Wanek

He died at different times in different places.
In Wales he died tomorrow,
which doesn't mean his death was preventable.
It had been coming for years,
crossing the ocean, the desert, pausing often,
moving like water or wind,
here turned aside by a stone,
then hurried where the way was clear.

Once I lay on my back in the grass and watched
as cloud after cloud moved east
and disintegrated. The mystery now
is not where they went, but how
I could ever have been so idle.

Funerals are all the same.
I saw him cry at his mother's wake
when I was young enough to be
picked up, lofted into someone's arms.
He, a man, cried that day,
but people smiled, too. You think now
you want to be remembered,
but the dead don't care.
My grandmother's face said that.

Indifference is a great relief, after a lifetime
of mothering one's many worries,
trying not to play favorites.

I wasn't present when he died.
I feel that keenly, that I should have
had a share. I was spared
unfairly. I was not fed
the bitter broth and the hard bread.
What time did it happen
exactly? What was I doing at that exact moment?
What can I do now?

But the moment is never exact.
One dies over years—yes, there is a first breath
and a last, yet consider a cut tulip
upright in a vase, closing as the day ends,
then turning toward the morning window, opening again.
One day I touch a petal and it falls off.
Even so the balding stem takes
another sip of water.

My mother held the phone to his ear
so each middle-aged child could say a distant good-bye,
and she searched his face for a sign.
Perhaps. No one knows what he heard
or if a phone was essential to it.
The longing to believe is more enduring
than any truth—truth is so perishable.
I once was found, but now I'm lost.
I could see, but now I'm blind.

APPLES

Michael Waters

for my father

I was the clumsy child
who stole apples
from your favorite tree
to toss them into the lake.

I have no excuse, but
those apples were never lost.
Each night, while you slept,
as apples bobbed in moonlight,

I waited in shallow water
until the apples washed ashore.
Each night I gave you an apple.
Sometimes I remember that desire

to take whatever belongs to you
so I can return it.
Now, on windless nights,
when the lake lies still,

I have another dream:
I gather you in my arms,
after death, and ease you
like a basketful of apples

into the moonlit water,
and we float home,
with an awkward grace,
to a continent dark with apples.

THE SMELL OF APPLES

Elizabeth Weir

Crab apples molder, thick as blood,
beneath our tree, the time of year
my mother used to come and stay.

In the heady scent of rot
she taught me how to make
apple glaze and Bakewell tarts;

I helped her bathe and dress.
Together we argued, talked and read
through the vinegar-sweet days.

She asked to stay in Minnesota,
far from England, but with me,
her only daughter. I wanted

to keep her, wanted to nurse
her slow decline, but we could not
insure a worn out English heart.

I had to send her home to die.
Now, in September, the tang
of fermenting apple flesh

trips a deep, familiar ache.
Thirsty for my mother,
I gulp the cider air.

Cemeteries

Sarah Brown Weitzman

About comfort
they think they know.

The long straight pity
of rows

suggests an order
to the cosmos.

A certain refutation
of sheer chance

lies in cropped grass
and denies

what weeds mean.
But when we gathered

over the green
of your grave, grief

churned it all back
into chaos.

VIGIL

Sarah Brown Weitzman

The moon's half-eaten tonight
like the yellow apple
you wanted
but could not finish
in your last sickness.
I have come again
to clean the moss from the rocks
that guard you
from wolves, my son,
though I know your spirit
is not here but climbs
among the silver web of stars
where you have the Dancing Bear
for a playmate and drink
from the Great Gourd
and perhaps forget us.
While your father sleeps
I come to do my work.
It is better
he does not know of this.
He is resigned
about the moss
that thrives
while the corn withers
and that parents survive
their children.
Before he wakes
I must be back.

The moon will make false
day of my return
but I am afraid
the way will be dark, dark.

FOR THE LAST ONE

Anthony Russell White

Let the lacrimatories be carved from jade and alabaster
to be filled with the tears of those who bury the dead.
Red Thunder Cloud is dead, and his cold lips grip
the last human link to the spoken Catawba language.

Just as the beekeeper was the first to master Everest,
there is always someone who is the last one,
even the last to speak an ancient tongue,
learned at a family hearth, mouthful by mouthful.

THE OCTOPUS

J.P. White

Maybe the short life of the octopus
is best as she clings to the cave wall.
In three years she gets three hearts
and spends them all. Her final act
before dying is to blow hatchlings

from her door. You might think
she recoils into too much darkness,
but with very little slippage, unlike
my father, eighty-nine now, repeating
bits of story into one non sequitur.

It hurts to watch him stagger into dotage,
when he claimed, like so many others,
he would never let this crimped, jabbering
man find him. A sailor all his life
in love with the buried lee rail, now

he withers at the slightest Florida snap.
Will yours be a short or long life?
Given the choice, nearly all lean
toward the long run, but is it best
when more is eventually much less?

I walk the beach to escape the cave
of his fuzzy brain, angry with myself
for my impatience with his patter.
I don't pan for the black shark's teeth
he asks about as if they were pearls

to buy him one more trick at the wheel.
Instead, I picture the octopus,
living out past the string of shrimpers
dragging their rusted iron doors,
her suction-cup arms holding fast

to the inky deep-sea ledges
but not for long or just long enough,
her last heart giving out as her young
spring free for the scramble, suck, pull
of this brief, beautiful corruption.

My father, come back, go on,
show me how to swim into the mossy,
barnacled cave of your dying.

Sărăcă Inima Mè (My Sorrowing Heart)

Steve Wilson
  outside Biertan, Romania

Hush, my heart. There is still the light

through the windows, fields that remember
you. Past the yellow church beside the forest,
hush. I've had to learn the ease of waiting.
Somewhere, in autumns, the songs grow surer
with waiting. You cannot hurry through
hurt. Quiet. Still. Slow, like those swallows
along the rooftops. Color upon a shawl.

World, loving its long evenings in silence.

THE DAY

Rosemary Winslow

And so I came to the day
after the spring
of loving my mother
after the summer of letting her go
under the limber pines
I lay on my back
arms stretching out
over me over the house
holding me to the blue sky
soft
how the green
melted and spread
over me and settled
fluid   mobile
the tight upraised
shoulders of my childhood
let loose their protection
settled
as the tense bands of
muscles had let go
in the spring
from against my
mother
and I had loved her then
without harm without wanting
her to be
anything she was not
and I was hardly noticeable

the movement of air barely touched
the ribbons of planks beneath me
and the blue-green tufted needles above
I was large   rich
I was gone

And not for awhile did I
rise up,
walk in the day.

HIS FUNERAL

Jeff Worley

My father was finally unconfused,
the noose of Alzheimer's snapped.
Around him the malodorous roses
and long shafts of lilies.

I squeezed his shoulder, patted it
like the flank of a favorite dog.
I knew this was a dumb, sentimental
gesture. I didn't care.

My sister said—the whole room listening—
that our father had gone now
to a better place. The funeral home
claque nodded like breeze-bent stalks.

I wished for a long moment my sister
was right, but then two men came
and closed the light from him.
His new roof screwed tightly down,

I could still hear him say, *A better place,
Joyce? Show me the evidence.* The organ
shook down dust from the oak beams.
Joyce sang loudly along on the first hymn
with the few people who'd come. In my head
I sang "Don't Fence Me In." Dad told me
he'd hummed this when the gates
of Stalag XI-B were flung open

and he hobbled out on makeshift crutches.
He was headed back to Kansas, its glorious
dullness and flatness, bars of sunshine
in his father's field, the amazing grace

of wheat and wheat and wheat.

CHLOE IN LATE JANUARY

David Young

Midwinter here, a frozen pause, and now
some nineteen years since cancer took your life.

This month's old god, they say, faced opposite directions,
backward and forward. May I do that, too?

It's much the same. Deer come and go, as soft
as souls in Hades, glimpsed at wood's edge toward dusk;
their tracks in daylight show they come at night
to taste my neighbor's crab trees, last fall's fruit
shrunk down to sour puckered berries.

And where, in this arrested world,
might I expect to meet your cordial spirit?

You would not bother with that graveyard, smooth
below its gleaming cloak of snow. You'd want
to weave among the trees, beside the tiny kinglet,
gold head aglow, warming itself
with ingenuities, adapting, singing,
borne on the major currents of this life
like the creek that surprised me yesterday again,
running full tilt across its pebbled bottom
even in this deep cold.

Each of Us Has a Name

Zelda
   Translated/adapted by Marcia Falk

Each of us has a name
given by the source of life
and given by our parents

Each of us has a name
given by our stature and our smile
and given by what we wear

Each of us has a name
given by the mountains
and given by our walls

Each of us has a name
given by the stars
and given by our neighbors

Each of us has a name
given by our sins
and given by our longing

Each of us has a name
given by our enemies
and given by our love

Each of us has a name
given by our celebrations
and given by our work

Each of us has a name

given by the seasons
and given by our blindness

Each of us has a name
given by the sea
and given by
our death.

Visiting the Alzheimer's Wing

Fredrick Zydek

She will not remember who I am
but will take the glass of ice and cola
with the same words with which I am
greeted each week: "Oh yes, I love

Coca Cola." She does remember
that. She will tell me stories of life
on the wing. She thinks she's living
at a hotel. She complains about maid

service, the skills of the chef, how poor
the performances are in the lounge
and that her husband, dead now these
many years, is off gambling somewhere

and probably pinching a cocktail
waitresses derriere as she speaks. She
will tell me there is something wrong
with most of the guests. "They're all

so old and forgetful," she'll complain.
"This is the last time I'm going to let
Frank book us into a hotel that caters
to the older generation. They're the

dullest damn people I've ever met."
I will avoid reminding her that Frank
was not her husband's name and show
her photographs from the old family

album. It won't help. She likes to look
at them because of the clothing styles
in the 30s and 40s. "Don't you wish
those trends would come back, John,"

she'll ask. I won't tell her my real name,
and force myself to remember that no
matter how hard I try or what I do,
I will never be her favorite nephew again.

BASHO

The temple bell stops,
but the sound keeps coming
out of the flowers.

NOTES ON CONTRIBUTORS

MARIAN AITCHES is a professor in the History Department at the University of Texas in San Antonio, Texas. She has completed her first chapbook, *Fishing for Light*, and is completing a full length manuscript.

DIANE AVERILL'S first book, *Branches Doubled Over With Fruit*, was published by the University of Florida Press. Her second collection, *Beautiful Obstacles*, was published by Blue Light Press. Both books were finalists for the Oregon Book Award. She is a graduate of the M.F.A. program at the University of Oregon and she teaches at Clackamas Community College.

CYNTHIA M. BAER is a writer and, for twenty-seven years, a teacher of writing and literature. For the last twenty years, she has made her home the Santa Cruz Mountains, where she is apprenticed to Nature, and the subtle graces of rock and tree and sky.

MARY JO BANG is the author of five books of poems including her most recent collection, *Elegy*, which traces the aftermath of her son's death. Wayne Koestenbaum writes: "Mary Jo Bang's remarkable elegies recall the late work of Ingeborg Bachmann—a febrile, recursive lyricism. Like Nietzsche or Plath, Bang flouts naysayers; luridly alive, she drives deep into aporia, her new, sad country. Her stanzas, sometimes spilling, sometimes severe, perform an uncanny death-song, recklessly extended—nearly to the breaking point." She lives in St. Louis, Missouri, where she is Professor of English and Director of the Creative Writing Program at Washington University.

COLEMAN BARKS is retired now from teaching at the University of Georgia for thirty years. A collection of his personal poems, *Winter Sky: New and Selected Poems*, 1968-2008 has just been published by the University of Georgia Press. Several of his Rumi translations are available through HarperOne, including the bestselling *Essential Rumi*.

JACKIE BARTLEY'S work has appeared in a number of journals, most recently, *Nimrod*, *Pinyon*, and *Calyx*. Her last collection, *Ordinary Time* (2007), won the Spire Press Poetry Prize. She teaches writing at Hope College in Holland, Michigan where she lives with her husband John.

BASHO (1644-1694) is the most famous poet of the Edo period in Japan. He is considered the master of haiku. Within Japan many of his poems are reproduced on monuments and historic sites.

MARVIN BELL was born in New York City. He has an M.A. from the University of Chicago and an M.F.A. from the University of Iowa. He was Iowa's first poet laureate. Bell has published sixteen books of poetry, and is currently a professor of literature at the University of Iowa. He has received Fullbrights, NEA Fellowships, and a Guggenheim.

CAL BENSON is a teacher turned poet and published *Peterpie Moon* in 2005, for the first anniversary of his son's death. In 2007, Calyx Press (Duluth, MN) published *Dakota Boy*, which received finalist awards from NEMBA and the Midwest Independent Publishers Association. He serves on the board of Lake Superior Writers in Duluth.

WENDELL BERRY was born in Kentucky. He has an M.A. in English from the University of Kentucky. In addition, he studied with Wallace Stegner at the University of California, Berkeley. A prolific poet, essayist, and fiction writer, Berry has taught at NYU's University College in the Bronx, and at the University of Kentucky. Berry has spend many years practicing his belief in sustainable farming. He has received both Guggenheim and Rockefeller Fellowships.

BARBARA BLATNER's work has appeared in *House Organ, HazMat*, and others; in a chapbook, *The Pope in Space* (Intertext Press) and on National Public Radio – a verse play for "Epiphany," *No Star Shines Sharper* (Baker's Plays). Her play, *Marilyn Monroe in the Desert*, was read recently at the Living Theatre.

GARY BOELHOWER is professor of Theology and Religious Studies at The College of Saint Scholastica in Duluth, Minnesota where he teaches courses in "Living, Dying and Grieving" and "Healthcare Ethics." His poetry has appeared in his book of poems and stories entitled *Sacred Times, Sacred Seasons* and in several journals and anthologies.

KATHLEEN SHEEDER BONANNO's autobiographical collection, *Slamming Open the Door* (the 2008 Beatrice Hawley Award winner), has been described by Sharon Olds as "a gift of power, truth, rage, and beauty." It is available from Alice James Books.

ANNIE BREITENBUCHER is a freelance writer living in Minneapolis; her stories have previously appeared in the *Minneapolis Star Tribune*, where she worked for twenty-three years. Her first poetry collection, *Fortune*, was published by the Laurel Poetry Collective in 2006.

NANCY BREWKA-CLARK has been published in many areas and in numerous genres, from plays to mysteries, but she finds poetry the most spiritually rewarding.

EMILY K. BRIGHT is the author of *Glances Back* (Pudding House Press, 2007). In 2008, she received her M.F.A. in poetry from the University of Minnesota. Originally from New England, she now teaches writing in Eau Claire, Wisconisn.

Joseph Bruchac is a storyteller and writer whose work often reflects his Abenaki ancestry. In addition, he is a much-published poet and also a popular children's author. He lives with his family in Greenfield Center, New York.

Christopher Buckley's sixteenth book of poetry, *Modern History: Prose Poems 1987-2007*, is published by Tupelo Press. *Bear Flag Republic: Prose Poems & Poetics from California*, edited with Gary Young, was published by Alcatraz Editions/Greenhouse Review Press in 2008. He was a Guggenheim Fellow in Poetry for 2007-2008, and was awarded the James Dickey Prize for 2008 from Five Points Magazine. He teaches in the creative writing program at the University of California, Riverside.

Andrea Hollander Budy, Writer-in-Residence at Lyon College, is the author of three poetry collections, most recently, *Woman in the Painting* (Autumn House, 2006). Her first book won the Nicholas Roerich Poetry Prize. Other awards include a Pushcart Prize for memoir and two fellowships from the National Endowment for the Arts.

Cullen Bailey Burns is the author of *Paper Boat* (New Rivers Press), a finalist for the 2004 Minnesota Book Awards. Her poems have appeared in *Denver Quarterly, Rattle, Water-Stone, Court Green*, and many other magazines. She lives in Minneapolis.

Sharon M. Carter was born in London, and has lived in Washington state since 1983, providing mental health services. She was a co-editor of *Literary Salt*, received a Hedgebrook residency in 2001, and was a Jack Straw writer in 2003.

Raymond Carver, Jr. (1938–1988) was an American short story writer and poet. Carver is considered a major American writer of the late 20th century and also a major force in the revitalization of the short story in the 1980s. His poem "Late Fragment," included in this anthology, was one of the last poems he wrote, and is collected in "A New Path to the Waterfall" (1989).

Sharon Chmielarz has had four books of poetry, one chapbook, and three children's books published. Her poems have been widely published and her book, *The Other Mozart*, has been made into a two-part opera. Its first performance was in Baton Rouge, as part of the Reader's Little Theatre Series, in January, 2009.

David Chura lives in Massachusetts and has published poetry in *The Anthology of New England Writers, Blueline, English Journal,* and *Essential Love*. His essay, "Pin-ups," was nominated for a 2005 Pushcart Prize. His short story, "Let a Woman in Your Life," was a finalist in the Glimmer Train "Family Matters" competition.

Lucille Clifton was born and raised in Depew, New York. She graduated from SUNY at Fredonia and has taught at Columbia University, George Washington University, the University of California Santa Cruz, and St. Mary's College, Maryland.

Clifton was the Poet Laureate of Maryland, 1979-1985. She has published twelve books of poetry, over twenty children's books, and a memoir. In 2007 Clifton received the Ruth Lilly Poetry Prize.

BILLY COLLINS was born in New York City, and later received both an M.A. and Ph.D. at the University of California, Riverside. From 2001-2003 he was the Poet Laureate of the United States. Collins is distinguished professor at Lehman College in the Bronx. He was *Poetry* magazine's "Poet of the Year" in 1994, and has received both NEA and Guggenheim Fellowships. He has published ten books of poetry.

DEBORAH GORDON COOPER has been published in numerous literary journals and anthologies. She is the author of four poetry chapbooks. Deborah has collaborated with musicians, dancers and visual artists, most frequently with her husband, Joel Cooper, a printmaker.

EDUARDO C. CORRAL's work has been honored with a "Discovery"/*The Nation* award and residencies from the MacDowell Colony and Yaddo. Currently, he's the Philip Roth Resident in Creative Writing at Bucknell University.

BARBARA CROOKER's *Radiance* won the 2005 Word Press First Book award, and was a finalist for the 2006 Paterson Poetry Prize. Her new book, *Line Dance*, is also from Word Press. She was the 2003 recipient of the Thomas Merton Poetry of the Sacred Award, and has received three fellowships in Literature from the Pennsylvania Council on the Arts.

FLORENCE CHARD DACEY lives in Cottonwood, Minnesota and has published three poetry collections: *The Swoon, The Necklace,* and *Maynard Went This Way. Rock Worn by Water* is forthcoming from Plain View Press. Her website is www.florencedacey.com.

PHILIP DACEY's latest of ten books is *Vertebrae Rosaries: Fifty Sonnets* (Red Dragonfly Press, 2008). His awards include a Fulbright Fellowship to Yugoslavia, two National Endowment for the Arts Creative Writing Fellowships, and three Pushcart prizes. His website is www.philipdacey.com.

TODD DAVIS, winner of the Gwendolyn Brooks Poetry Prize, is the author of two books of poems *Ripe* (Bottom Dog Press, 2002) and *Some Heaven* (Michigan State University Press, 2007). Poems from *Some Heaven* have been featured on Garrison Keillor's *The Writer's Almanac* and in Ted Kooser's "American Life in Poetry."

DIANA DER-HOVANESSIAN, American born poet, is the author of twenty-three books of poetry and translations, winner of prizes from *American Scholar, Prairie Schooner, Yankee,* et al. She has received the Paterson Poetry Prize and awards from the National Endowment for the Arts. She was twice a Fulbright professor of American literature.

BLAGA DIMITROVA (1922-2003) was a Bulgarian poet and also Vice-President of Bulgaria from 1992-1993. As a poet, she was often criticized by the government for not being "politically correct." She was the inspiration for John Updike's story, "The Bulgarian Poetess."

W. D. EHRHART's most recent collection of poems is *Sleeping with the Dead* (Adastra Press, 2006). He lives in Philadelphia with his wife Anne and daughter Leela, and teaches English and history at the Haverford School.

ALAN ELYSHEVITZ is a poet and short story writer from East Norriton, PA. His published work includes two poetry chapbooks: *The Splinter in Passion's Paw* (New Spirit) and *Theory of Everything* (Pudding House). He currently teaches English at the Community College of Philadelphia.

MARCIA FALK is a poet, translator, and Judaic scholar. She is the author of several highly acclaimed books, including *The Book of Blessings: New Jewish Prayers for Daily Life, the Sabbath, and the New Moon Festival; The Song of Songs: Love Lyrics from the Bible; The Spectacular Difference: Selected Poems of Zelda; With Teeth in the Earth: Selected Poems of Malka Heifetz Tussman;* and three books of her own poetry, *This Year in Jerusalem, It Is July in Virginia* and *My Son Likes Weather*. Her website is www.marciafalk.com.

TERESA BOYLE FALSANI, a native of Portland, Maine, moved to Duluth, Minnesota in 1973. A retired English teacher and freelance writer, she serves on the Advisory Boards of Lake Superior Writers and the Duluth Woman's Health Center. Her writing appears in *Dust & Fire, English Journal, Arthuriana* and other publications.

MARA FAULKNER, OSB, is a member of the Benedictine monastery in St. Joseph, MN, and teaches literature and writing at the College of St. Benedict/St. John's University. Besides poetry, she has written three books, most recently *Going Blind: A Memoir* (forthcoming from SUNY Press.)

TESS GALLAGHER was born in Port Angeles, Washington. She studied at the University of Washington under Theodore Roethke. She also received an M.F.A. from the University of Iowa. Gallagher is the author of ten books of poetry, in addition to fiction and essays. She has received two NEA awards and a Guggenheim Fellowship.

JANE GRAHAM GEORGE is the author of *Aotearoa: New Zealand Poems* and *Library Land*, both published by Red Dragonfly Press. Her poems have appeared in *Poetry Australia, the Auroean,* and *Country Lines: 87 Minnesota Counties, 130 Minnesota Poets*. She currently lives in the Twin Cities (Minnesota) where she works as a librarian.

LAURA CRAFTON GILPIN (1950-2007) was a poet, nurse, and passionate advocate for patient's rights. She was born in Wisconsin but moved to Indianapolis, Indiana in 1955. After graduating from the local public school system, she attended Sarah Lawrence College, graduating with a B.A. in 1972 and Columbia University's School of the Arts in New York City with her M.F.A. in 1974. Laura was chosen by juror and poet William Stafford to receive the Walt Whitman Award in 1976. The award was created to assist poets publishing a first book. She was its second recipient. Her first book, *The Hocus-Pocus of the Universe* was published by Doubleday.

LINDA GLASER writes: "Often during times of loss, I have turned to poetry and other forms of writing for comfort, nourishment, deep understanding, and connection. After my father's death, my poem 'After' gave me that opportunity—for which I am deeply grateful."

JANE ELLEN GLASSER's poetry has appeared in *The Hudson Review, The Southern Review,* and *The Georgia Review.* Her second book, *Light Persists,* won the Tampa Review Prize for Poetry in 2005. Her grief poems impose meaning on the incomprehensible—the death of her daughter at age twenty-two.

VICKI GRAHAM is the author of two poetry collections: *The Tenderness of Bees,* 2008, and *Alembic,* a finalist for the Minnesota Book Award, 2001. Her poems have appeared in *Poetry, Midwest Quarterly, Seneca Review, Water-Stone,* and other journals, and in the anthologies *To Sing Along the Way* and *County Lines.*

MARJ HAHNE considers herself first a teacher, then a poet, having taught poetry writing, high school mathematics, English-as-a-second-Language, and Business English. Marj has performed and taught poetry at over 100 venues around the country, including public radio and television. Her website is www.marjhahne.com.

JOY HARJO was born in Tulsa, Oklahoma and is a member of the Muscogee (Creek) Nation of Oklahoma. She is a graduate of the Iowa Writers' Workshop. Harjo has written nine books of poetry and a children's book. She plays tenor sax for the band, "Poetic Justice."

PENNY HARTER is widely published in anthologies and journals. Among a number of collections, her most recent book is *The Night Marsh.* She won three poetry fellowships from the New Jersey State Council on the Arts and the Mary Carolyn Davies Award from the Poetry Society of America.

MARGARET HASSE, originally from South Dakota, makes her home in Saint Paul, Minnesota. She was educated at Stanford University and the University of Minnesota. She's the author of three poetry collections: *Stars Above, Stars Below; In a Sheep's Eye, Darling;* and *Milk and Tides* (Nodin Press, 2008.)

NAOMI HAUGEN is currently an M.F.A. student at Hamline University. She writes and teaches music in Hayward, Wisconsin and Saint Paul, Minnesota.

SUSAN CAROL HAUSER is the author of twelve books including *Outside After Dark:*

New and Selected Poems. She received two Minnesota Book Awards and a Jerome Foundation Travel and Study Grant. She has an M.F.A. From Bowling Green State University, Ohio. She teaches at Bemidji State University. Her website is www.susanhauser.com.

LORRAINE HEALY is an Argentinean poet who lives on Whibey Island, Washington. Nominated for a Pushcart Prize in 2004, she has been published extensively. A graduate from the New England College M.F.A. and Antioch University Los Angeles post-M.F.A. Programs, she has published two chapbooks. Her full-length manuscript is looking for a publisher.

BOB HICOK was born in Michigan, where he owned and operated an automotive die design business. He has written five books of poetry, and his poems have appeared in many prestigious periodicals such as *The New Yorker, Paris Review,* and *Poetry.* Hicok is an Associate Professor of Creative Writing at Virginia Technical Institute.

BILL HOLM (1943-2009) was born and raised in Minneota, Minnesota. He was a poet, essayist, memoirist, and musician. Holm was the author of nearly a dozen books, including *The Heart Can Be Filled Anywhere on Earth, Coming Home Crazy, Playing the Black Piano, Eccentric Islands* and *The Windows of Brimmes: An American in Iceland.* He was the recipient of the Cobb Partnership Award, which honors Americans who have contributed to strengthening bilateral relations with Iceland.

PAUL HOSTOVSKY's poems have been featured on "Poetry Daily," "Verse Daily," and "The Writer's Almanac." He has won a Pushcart Prize, the Muriel Craft Bailey Award from The Comstock Review, and chapbook contests from Grayson Books, Riverstone Press, and Frank Cat Press. His first full-length collection, *Bending the Notes,* is available from Main Street Rag.

DAVID IGNATOW (1914-1997) wrote over twenty five books of lyric and prose poems. His first volume was *Poems* (1948); his final collection was *Living Is What I Wanted: Last Poems* (1999). He received many awards, including the Robert Frost Medal, the Bollingen Prize, and the John Steinbeck Award, as well as two Guggenheim fellowships. He was the editor of several literary journals, and poetry editor of *The Nation.* He served as poet-in-residence and professor at several colleges and universities, including Columbia University.

JANET JERVE writes for a nonprofit organization. Her poems have appeared in *Poetry East, Water-Stone Review, Great River Review, Hurricane Alice, Lake Effect* and *A Ghost at Heart's Edge,* an anthology on adoption published by North Atlantic Books. She has two children and lives with her husband in Minneapolis.

SHEILA GOLBURGH JOHNSON was fortunate to have studied poetry with former British Poet Laureate Ted Hughes when she was a student in the early 1960s. She has won local, national, and international awards for her poetry.

DEBORAH KEENAN is the author of eight collections of poetry. The latest, *Willow Room, Green Door: New and Selected Poems*, from Milkweed Editions, received the Minnesota Book Award for poetry in 2008. She is a professor and faculty advisor at Hamline University in the School of Graduate Liberal Studies, in beautiful St. Paul, Minnesota.

JANE KENYON (1947-1995) was born in Ann Arbor, Michigan, where she lived until she moved to Eagle Pond Farm in New Hampshire, her home for the remainder of her life. Her published works include five volumes of poetry, including *Otherwise: New and Selected Poems*, and *A Hundred White Daffodils: Essays, the Akhmatova Translations, Newspaper Columns, Notes, Interviews, and One Poem*. She was the New Hampshire poet laureate at the time of her death.

C. L. KNIGHT is the associate director of Anhinga Press, where she designs and edits books. Her poetry has appeared in *Louisiana Literature, Tar River Review, Earth's Daughters, The Ledge, Slipstream, Comstock Review, Epicenter,* and *Redactions*. She is the co-editor of *Snakebird: Thirty Years of Anhinga Poets*.

TED KOOSER spent over thirty five years in the insurance industry supporting his poetry writing. He has published ten collections of poetry, including *Delights and Shadows*, and *Flying at Night: Poems 1965-1985*. He has also written two collections of essays, *Local Wonders: Seasons in the Bohemian Alps* and *Poetry Home Repair Manual: Practical Advice for Beginning Poets*. Kooser was Poet Laureate of the United States in 2004. He is a visiting professor at the University of Nebraska.

MAXINE KUMIN is a poet, children's author, fiction writer, and essayist. She has written eleven books of poetry, including *Up Country: Poems of New England,* for which she was awarded the Pulitzer Prize. Other awards include the American Academy of Arts and Letters award and the Levinson Prize. She lives in a farmhouse in rural New Hampshire.

JULIE LANDSMAN'S first love is poetry. She reads poems before she begins her fiction and nonfiction work in order to hold in her mind the beauty and clarity of language. She has published three memoirs and short stories and feels especially grateful for the chance to send an occasional poem into the world.

CHARLENE LANGFUR attended the Syracuse University Graduate Writing Program and now teaches at the College of the Desert. She is an organic gardener and lives in Palm Springs, California.

LI-YOUNG LEE was born in Indonesia to Chinese parents. The family moved to the United States in 1964. Lee has published four books of poetry, including *Book of Our Nights* (which won the 2002 William Carlos Williams award) and *Behind My Eyes*. He has also written a memoir, *The Winged Seed: A Remembrance*. He has received many awards and honors, including fellowships from the Academy of American Poets and the Guggenheim Foundation. He currently lives in Chicago, Illinois.

VICKY LETTMANN's poetry, essays, and fiction have appeared in *Twenty-six Minnesota Writers, Anna's House, A View from the Loft, Speakeasy, The Ruminator Review,* and other publications. *The Beach* is a collection of her poems with artwork by her mother. She is also a recipient of a Loft-McKnight Fellowship.

DENISE LEVERTOV (1923-1997) was born in England and had a prolific career as a poet, translator, editor and educator. She came to the United States in 1948 and published her first American collection of poems *Here and Now.* Among her other volumes are *Breathing the Water, With Eyes at the Back of Our Heads, Evening Train* and *Sands of the Well.*

ERIC LOCHBRIDGE is a poet and editor from Rapid City, South Dakota. He is the author of *Father's Curse* (Foothills Publishing, 2007), and the founding editor of After Long Busyness: A Poetry Blog (http://ericedits.wordpress.com).

DONNA J. LONG has published in *The Louisville Review, North American Review, Puerto Del Sol, The Florida Review, The Portland Review* and other journals. She is an associate professor of English at Fairmont State University. Long lost her mother, a smoker for thirty years, to lung cancer in 1985.

AUDRE LORDE (1934-1992) was the author of ten volumes of poetry and five works of prose. She was named New York Sate Poet in 1991; her other honors include the Manhattan Borough President's Award for Excellence in the Arts. *The Marvelous Arithmetics of Distance* was nominated for a National Book Critics Circle Award in 1994.

CHRISTINA LOVIN is the author of *What We Burned for Warmth* and *Little Fires.* An award-winning poet, her work is widely published and anthologized. She is the recipient of grants from the Kentucky Arts Council (including an Al Smith Fellowship) and the Kentucky Foundation for Women.

RAYMOND LUCZAK (raymondluczak.com) is the author and editor of ten books, two of which are poetry: *St. Michael's Fall* (Deaf Life Press, 1996) and *This Way to the Acorns* (The Tactile Mind Press, 2002.) A filmmaker and a playwright, he lives in Minneapolis, Minnesota.

MARJORIE MADDOX has published eight collections of poetry and over 300 poems, stories, and essays in journals and anthologies. She is Director of Creative Writing at Lock Haven University, co-editor of *Common Wealth: Contemporary Poets on Pennsylvania,* and author of two children's books from Boyd Mills Press. Her short story collection, *What She Was Saying,* was one of three finalists for the Katherine Anne Porter Book Award. Marjorie lives with her husband and two children in Williamsport, PA.

anthologies, including *Times of Sorrow, Times of Grace* (The Backwaters Press, 2002) and *Claiming the Spirit Within* (Beacon Press, 1996.)

KATHLEEN MCGOOKEY's poems and translations have appeared in over forty journals including *The Antioch Review, Boston Review, Epoch, Field, Indiana Review, The Laurel Review, Ploughshares, The Prose Poem: An International Journal, Quarterly West, Seneca Review, West Branch,* and *Willow Springs.* Her book is *Whatever Shines* (White Pine Press, 2001.) Her website is www.kathleenmcgookey.com.

ANN MCGOVERN has embraced poetry after forty-five years as an author of fifty-five children's books, including *Stone Soup.* Her sixty poems have been published in journals such as *Nimrod, Confrontation,* and *Georgetown Review.* Her recent chapbook, *Drawing Outside the Lines,* will be published by Finishing Line Press. She lives in New York City.

ETHNA MCKIERNAN's first book, *Caravan,* was a 1990 Minnesota Book Award nominee. Her poem included in this anthology, "Potatoes," is part of a suite of poems written about her mother's Alzheimer's disease, and appears in her second book, *The One Who Swears You Can't Start Over* (2002). McKiernan is a street outreach worker to the homeless in Minneapolis.

ERIK K. MORTENSON works as an English teacher when he's not writing poetry or book reviews. His work appears widely both in print and on-line. He was the 2008 recipient of the Leslie Leeds Poetry Prize. He lives in Connecticut with his wife, son, and two cats.

LISEL MUELLER was born in Hamburg, Germany in 1924. She is the author of a number of poetry collections, including *The Private Life, The Need to Hold Still* (winner of a National Book Award), and *Alive Together,* which won the Pulitzer Prize. She lives in Lake County, Illinois.

MATTHEW NADELSON is an English instructor at Riverside Community College. His poems have appeared in *Byline, Beauty Truth, Arocet, Ars Medica, Whistling Shade,* and other journals.

PABLO NERUDA (1904-1973) was born in Chile and became a poetic voice for the people of his country. His work has been widely translated. Neruda also served as a diplomat in posts in Europe and the Far East. In 1971, he was awarded the Nobel Prize in Literature. Pablo Neruda died in 1973, shortly after the coup in Chile which ousted Allende.

NAOMI SHIHAB NYE's Palestinian grandmother Sitti Khadra Shihab Idais Al-Zer lived to be 106 years old in the West Bank village of Sinjil.

PATRICIA O'DONNELL has had her writing published in many journals and anthologies, including *The New Yorker.* She directs the B.F.A. Program at the University of Maine,

Farmington, and lives in Wilton with her husband and daughter.

Sharon Olds was born in California. She published her first book of poetry *Satan Says* at the age of thirty-seven. Her work has won several prestigious prizes, including the National Book Critics Award for the volume *The Dead and the Living*. She lives in New York City.

Mary Oliver was born in Ohio in 1935. She is the author of seventeen volumes of poetry and six works of prose. She has won both the National Book Award and the Pulitzer Prize for poetry. Her collections include *Red Bird, Our World, Thirst* and *At Blackwater Pond*. She lives in Provincetown, Massachusetts.

Sheila Packa has a new book, *The Mother Tongue*, published by Calyx Press (Duluth, 2007). She's received two Loft-McKnight Fellowships and the ARAC Fellowships. Her work is featured in *To Sing Along the Way: Minnesota Women Poets from Pre-Territorial Days to the Present*, edited by Joyce Sutphen, Thom Tammaro, and Connie Wanek (New Rivers Press, 2006). Her website is www.sheilapacka.com.

Nancy Paddock lives and gardens in Litchfield, Minnesota. Her poems have appeared in many journals and anthologies, including *To Sing Along the Way* and *County Lines. Trust the Wild Heart* (Red Dragonfly Press) was a finalist for the 2006 Minnesota Book Award in Poetry. Chapters from her memoir-in-progress were included in *Stardust and Fate: The Blueroad Reader*.

Linda Pastan was born in New York City in 1932. Pastan began publishing poetry in the 1970s. She served as Poet Laureate of Maryland from 1991 to 1994. Among her twelve poetry books are *PM/AM*: New and Selected Poems and *Carnival Evening*: New and Selected Poems, both finalists for the National Book Award. Her most recent collection is *Queen of a Rainy Country*. She lives in Potomac, Maryland.

Roger Pfingston is a retired teacher of English and photography. Much of his work can be found on-line at such e-zines as *Mannequin Envy, Poetry Midwest*, and the *Innisfree Poetry Journal*. He is the recipient of the NEA Creative Writing Fellowship in Poetry.

Marge Piercy is the author of seventeen poetry collections including *Colors Passing Through Us, What Are Big Girls Made Of?, The Art of Blessing the Day: Poems with a Jewish Theme*, and most recently *The Crooked Inheritance*—all from Alfred A. Knopf. She has written seventeen novels, most recently *Sex Wars* from Morrow/Harper Collins, who also published her memoir, *Sleeping with Cats*.

Andrea Potos is the author of the poetry collections *Yaya's Cloth* (Iris Press) and *The Perfect Day* (Parallel Press). Her poems appear widely in journals and anthologies. She lives in Madison, Wisconsin with her husband and daughter.

Judith E. Prest, Duanesburg, New York, is a poet, collage artist, social worker and creativity coach. Her writing has appeared in *Earth's Daughters, Bereavement, Mad Poets Review, Slightly West, Writing For Our Lives, Enlightening Bolt* and in two anthologies—*Peer Glass* and *Layers of Possibility*.

ALASTAIR REID (born 1926) is a poet and a scholar of South American literature from Galloway in Scotland. He is known for his lighthearted style of poems and for his translations of South American poets Jorge Luis Borge and Pablo Neruda. He has lived in Spain, Switzerland, Greece, Morocco, throughout Latin America, and in the United States, where he has been employed by *The New Yorker* magazine.

CARLOS REYES is a noted poet, translator, and writer from Portland, Oregon. His most recent poetry book is *At The Edge of the Western Wave* (2004). Forthcoming is a book of translations: *La señal del cuervo/ The Sign of the Crow* by Mexican poet Ignacio Ruiz Pérez. He is at work on his "New & Selected." Reyes was recently honored with a Heinrich Boll Fellowship which included a two week writing residency on Achill Island, Ireland.

ADRIENNE RICH'S most recent books of poetry are *Telephone Ringing in the Labyrinth*: Poems 2004-2006 and *The School Among the Ruins*: 2000-2004. A selection of her essays, *Arts of the Possible: Essays and Conversations*, appeared in 2001. She edited Muriel Rukeyser's *Selected Poems* for the Library of America. In Spring 2009, Norton will publish *A Human Eye: Essays on Art in Society*. She is a recipient of the National Book Foundation's 2006 Medal for Distinguished Contribution to American Letters, among other honors. She lives in California.

SUSAN RICH lives in Seattle, Washington. She has received awards from the Academy of American Poets and PEN USA. Her books, *Cures Include Travel* and *The Cartographer's Tongue* are both published by White Pine Press. Recent poems appear in *The Gettysburg Review, Poetry Ireland*, and *New England Review*. Her next book is *The Alchemist's Kitchen*.

RAINER MARIA RILKE (1875–1926) is considered one of the German language's greatest 20th century poets. His haunting images focus on the difficulty of communion with the ineffable in an age of disbelief, solitude, and profound anxiety—themes that tend to position him as a transitional figure between the traditional and the modernist poets. His two most famous verse sequences are the *Sonnets to Orpheus* and the *Duino Elegies*; his two most famous prose works are the *Letters to a Young Poet*, and the semi-autobiographical *The Notebooks of Malte Laurids Brigge*.

GAIL RIXEN is the author of *Pictures of Three Seasons* (New Rivers Press), *Chicken Logic* (Sidewalks), and *Living on Dew* (Nebish Clay Press). She owns a small farm in northern Minnesota.

GEORGE ROBERTS continues to believe in the unnameable magic of poetry; that wherever one thing stands, another stands beside it.

HELEN RUGGIERI lives in Orleans, New York and has had work published recently in *The Mom Egg* and *Earth's Daughters*.

JELALUDDIN RUMI (1207-1273) is considered by many to be the world's greatest mystical poet. His language is Persian. The poetry sprang spontaneously from the inner work he was doing with a dervish learning community in Konya, Turkey. The poem included in this anthology is an elegy for someone in that community, whose name is not given.

KAY RYAN received bachelor's and master's degrees in English from University of California, Los Angeles. Her work went nearly unrecognized until the mid 1990s, when some of her poems were anthologized and the first reviews in national journals were published. She became widely recognized following her receipt of the Ruth Lilly Poetry Prize in 2004. In July, 2008, Ryan was selected as the sixteenth Poet Laureate Consultant to the Library of Congress.

EDITH RYLANDER has written in central Minnesota since 1964. She has received awards from the Bush and Loft-McKnight Foundations. Her books are *Rural Routes; Journeying Earthward; Dancing Back the Cranes;* and *Hive Dancer.*

KENNETH SALZMANN is a freelance writer and poet whose work appears in such publications as *Rattle, Sow's Ear Poetry Review, Riverine: An Anthology of Hudson Valley Writers, The Comstock Review,* and elsewhere. He lives in upstate New York with his wife, editor Sandi Gelles-Cole, and has one son, Joshua, a historian in Chicago.

MAY SARTON (1912-1995) was a poet, novelist, and memorist born in Wondelgem, Belgium. Three years later her family moved to Massachusetts. In 1945 she met her partner for the next thirteeen years, Judy Matlack, in Santa Fe, New Mexico. They separated when Sarton's father died and she moved to New Hampshire. Sarton lectured at various universities, including Harvard and Wellesley College. At her death, she had written fifty-three books.

LARRY SCHUG works as a recycling coordinator at the College of Saint Benedict in St. Joseph, Minnesota. He has published five poetry books, including *Arrogant Bones* with North Star Press (St. Cloud, Minnesota). He lives with his wife, two cats and one dog in St. Wendell Township, Minnesota.

NOELLE SICKELS is the author of the historical novels *Walking West, The Shopkeeper's Wife,* and, recently, *The Medium,* about a psychic on the World War II home front. She's had poems, essays, and stories published in anthologies and journals. Her story, "In Domestic Service," won an annual fiction award from *Zone 3.*

JAMES SIEGEL'S prose and poetry have recently appeared in or are forthcoming from *The Modern Review, The Oklahoma Review, Paterson Literary Review, The New York Times, The Cherry Blossom Review,* and *Cairn.* He holds an M.F.A. from

The Modern Review, The Oklahoma Review, Paterson Literary Review, The New York Times, The Cherry Blossom Review, and *Cairn*. He holds an M.F.A. from Stonecoast at USM and a B.F.A. from Brooklyn College. He lives in Portland, Maine with his wife and greyhound. He teaches at Brunswick High School.

ANNE SIMPSON has been a caregiver for her husband Bob for fifteen years. They moved from Duluth, Minnesota to Saint Paul four years ago to provide him with the Alzheimer's facility he needed. She commutes once a month from Saint Paul to Duluth, to meet with her poets' group.

FLOYD SKLOOT'S seven poetry collections include *Selected Poems: 1970-2005* (Tupelo Press, 2008) and *The Snow's Music* (LSU Press, 2008). He is also an essayist and novelist. Skloot has won three Pushcart Prize awards, the PEN USA Literary Award, and an Independent Publishers Book Award. He lives in Portland, Oregon.

EMILY LOUISE SMITH'S poems have appeared in *Columbia Poetry Review, The Journal, Smartish Pace,* and *Tar River Poetry,* among others. A former HUB-BUB Writers in Residence and Byington Fellow at the University of North Carolina Wilmington, she currently directs UNCW's literary book imprint, "The Publishing Laboratory," and teaches publishing arts.

RAY AND MARA SMITH (NOW MARA HART), poet and librarian, translated many Spanish poets, and especially loved Pablo Neruda.

JOSEPH A. SOLDATI has published three poetry collections, and has had poems and essays published in regional and national magazines, journals, e-zines, and anthologies, including *The Litchfield Review, The Enignatist, Writers' Dojo, Margie: The American Journal of Poetry,* and *Line Drives: 100 Contemporary Baseball Poems.* He lives in Portland, Oregon.

RICHARD SOLLY is the senior editor at Hazelden Publishing. His most recent book of poetry is *From Where the Rivers Come* (Holy Cow! Press, 2007).

WILLIAM STAFFORD (1914-1993) published sixty books of poetry and prose, including *Traveling through the Dark,* which won the National Book Award in 1963. He taught at Lewis & Clark College, and traveled as a witness for literature and peace. He was Poetry Consultant to the Library of Congress—a position now known as the Poet Laureate.

BARRY STERNLIEB'S work appears in *Poetry, The Southern Review, Virginia Quarterly Review, Gettysburg Review, Commonweal, New England Review,* and others. In addition to receiving a 2004 Massachusetts Cultural Council Fellowship in Poetry, he edits Mad River Press, specializing in handmade limited edition letterpress chapbooks and prints since 1986.

ANNE STEWART currently lives in the north woods of Minnesota where she is regularly website is www.annestewart.info.

MYRNA STONE is the author of two full-length poetry collections, *How Else to Love the World* and *The Art of Loss*. Her poems have appeared in *Poetry, TriQuarterly,* and *Ploughshares*, among others. She has received fellowships from the Ohio Arts Council and Vermont Studio Center.

THOM TAMMARO lives and works in Moorhead, Minnesota. He is the author of two full-length collections of poems, *Holding on for Dear Life* and *When the Italians Come to My Home Town*, and two chapbooks, *31 Mornings in December* and *Minnesota Suite*.

NATASHA TRETHEWEY was born in Gulfport, Mississippi, in 1966. She earned an M.A. in poetry from Hollins University and M.F.A. in poetry from the University of Massachusetts. Her first collection of poetry, *Domestic Work* (2000), was selected by Rita Dove as the winner of the inaugural Cave Canem Poetry Prize for the best first book by an African American poet. Since then, she has published two more collections of poetry, including *Native Guard* (Houghton Mifflin, 2006), which received the Pulitzer Prize for Poetry, and *Bellocq's Ophelia* (2002). She is Professor of English at Emory University where she holds the Phillis Wheatley Distinguished Chair in Poetry.

CLAUDIA VAN GERVEN lives in Boulder, Colorado where she teaches writing. Her poems have appeared in numerous magazines and journals, as well as anthologies. She has won several national prizes. Her chapbook, *The Ends of Sunbonnet Sue,* won the Angelfish Press Prize.

SHERRE VERNON mourns the loss of her brother, Christopher Sellers. She lives, writes, and teaches in Los Angeles.

MARK VINZ is Professor Emeritus of English at Minnesota State University, Moorhead. His creative work has appeared in numerous magazines and anthologies; his most recent book is *Long Distance*, a collection of poems. He is also the co-editor of several anthologies, including *Inheriting the Land: Contemporary Voices from the Midwest.*

DAVI WALDERS' poetry and prose have appeared in more than 200 anthologies and journals. She developed and directs the Vital Signs Writing Project at NIH in Bethesda, Maryland, which is funded by The Witter Bynner Foundation for Poetry. Her work has been choreographed and performed in New York City and elsewhere, read by Garrison Keillor on The Writer's Almanac, and nominated for a Pushcart Prize.

STEPHANIE WALKER'S poems have appeared in *Poet Lore, Gulf Coast, Southern Humanities Review, Hiram Poetry Review,* among other journals. She works in marketing at an independent bookstore in Boulder, Colorado.

Humanities Review, Hiram Poetry Review, among other journals. She works in marketing at an independent bookstore in Boulder, Colorado.

CATHERINE SENNE WALLACE'S poems have appeared in numerous journals and magazines as well as CD recordings. A former English teacher, ad agency account executive, and communications consultant, she teaches in the autism spectrum program in an Edina, Minnesota middle school. She lives in Minneapolis with one husband and one perfect cat.

JENNIFER WALLACE teaches at Maryland Institute, College of Art in Baltimore. She is a poetry editor at The Cortland Review and a founding editor of Toadlily Press. Her poems have been featured in *Barrow Street, Lilliput Review, The Potomac Review, The Worchester Review, Zone 3* and on public radio.

CONNIE WANEK is the author of *Bonfire* (1997) and *Hartley Field* (2002). Her new book of poems, *On Speaking Terms,* is forthcoming from Copper Canyon Press in 2009. She was a Witter Bynner Fellow of the Library of Congress in 2006. She lives in Duluth, Minnesota.

MICHAEL WATERS' recent books include *Darling Vulgarity* (2006—finalist for the Los Angeles Times Book Prize) and *Parthenopi:* New and Selected Poems (2001) from BOA Editions, as well as *Contemporary American Poetry* (2006) from Houghton Mifflin. He teaches at Monmouth University in New Jersey and in the Dew University M.F.A. Program.

ELIZABETH WEIR is a SASE/Jerome Award winner and has been a finalist for the Loft Mentor Series in poetry. Her poetry has been published in *American Poetry Quarterly, White Pelican Review, Sidewalks, ArtWord Quarterly, Voices for the Land, Water-Stone, Out of Line, Alimentum,* and *Main Channel Voices.*

SARAH BROWN WEITZMAN has had over 200 poems published in numerous writing journals including *The North American Review, American Writing, Potomac Review, America.* Her second chapbook, *The Forbidden* (2003, Pudding House) was followed by *Never Far from Flesh,* a full-length volume of poems (Main Street Rag, 2005). Weitzman received a National Endowment for the Arts Fellowship, was a finalist in the Academy of American Poets' Walt Whitman Award twice, and more recently was a finalist for The Foley Prize in 2003. A former New York academic, Weitzman is retired and lives in Florida.

ANTHONY RUSSELL WHITE'S poetic high point was a visit to the tomb of Jelaluddin Rumi at Konya, Turkey—he is still awed by Rumi's poetry. William Stafford has been another major influence for White; he admires Stafford's quiet, plain language which manages to go quite deep in a few lines.

J. P. WHITE is the author of four books of poems, including *The Pomegranate Tree Speaks from the Dictator's Garden* (Holy Cow! Press). His debut novel, *Every Boat*

Journal, Commonweal, North American Review, America, Christian Science Monitor, Blue Unicorn, New Orleans Review, New Letters as well as in anthologies including *O Taste and See: Food Poems, Visiting Frost: Poems Inspired by Robert Frost, Like Thunder: Poets Respond to Violence in America*. His books include *Allegory Dance* and *Singapore Express*. He teaches at Texas State University.

ROSEMARY WINSLOW's work has appeared in *32 Poems, Poet Lore, The Southern Review, Beltway Poetry Journal, Locus Point*, and many other journals, and in several anthologies. Her book *Green Bodies* was published by Word Works in 2007. She has received three Larry Neal Awards, and grants from the District of Columbia Arts Commission and the Vermont Studio Center. She lives and works in Washington, D.C., and New Hampshire.

JEFF WORLEY has published three collections of poetry, the most recent entitled *Happy Hour at the Two Keys Tavern* (Mid-List Press, 2006). His poems have appeared in *The Threepenny Review, The Georgia Review, New England Review, Shenandoah,* and *The Southern Review*. The poem included in this anthology, "His Funeral," won the *Atlanta Review's* 2002 International Poetry Competition.

DAVID YOUNG has published ten books of poetry since 1968, when his first collection, *Sweating Out the Winter,* won the United States Award of the International Poetry Forum. His newest collection, published in February 2006, is *Black Lab* (Knopf).

ZELDA SCHNEURSON MISHKOVSKY (1914-1984) was an Orthodox Jew descended from a line of prominent Hasidic rabbis, who emerged from the world of her fathers and mothers to become a best-selling author beloved by the diverse Israeli readership. Her poetry is imbued with deep faith, free of the doubt and irony that sometimes permeates the work of other modern Hebrew poets.

FREDERICK ZYDECK is the author of eight poetry collections. Formerly a professor of creative writing and theology at the University of Nebraska and later at the College of Saint Mary, he is now a gentleman farmer when he isn't writing. He is the editor for Lone Willow Press.

PERMISSIONS AND SOURCES

We wish to express our thanks to authors, translators and other copyright holders for permission to include the works indicated below. Every effort has been made to identify copyright holders and obtain reprint permission.

"The Role of Elegy," by Mary Jo Bang, copyright © 2007 by Mary Jo Bang. Reprinted from *Elegy* with the permission of Graywolf Press, Saint Paul, Minnesota.

"Ghazel for My Mother," by Janice Bartley, first appeared in the *North American Review*. Reprinted by permission of the author.

"Ritual #3," by Cal Benson, first appeared in *Dakota Boy* (Calyx Press, Duluth, MN, 2007). Reprinted by permission of the author.

"The Wish to Be Generous," by Wendell Berry, from *Selected Poems of Wendell Berry* (Counterpoint, 1999), copyright © 1999, reprinted by permission.

"Urgency," by Annie Breitenbucker, previously appeared in *Fortune*, copyright © 2006 by Annie Breitenbucker (Laurel Poetry Collective, 2006). Reprinted by permission of the author.

"The day before you died...," by Emily K. Bright, is reprinted from *Glances Back* (Pudding House Press, 2007) by permission of the author.

"To Ernesto Trejo in the Other World," by Christopher Buckley, is reprinted from *Sky* (Sheep Meadow Press, New York) copyright © 2004 Christopher Buckley by permission of the author.

"Poem in October," by Andrea Hollander Budy, is reprinted from *Woman in the Painting* (Autumn Hose Press) copyright © 2006 Andrea Hollander Budy, by permission of Autumn House Press and the author.

"Maple Tress and Unexpected Snow," by Cullen Baily Burns, first appeared in *Water-Stone Review*, Volume II, reprinted by permission of the author.

"Cradle," by Sharon Carter, is reprinted from "Poetry on the Buses" (Seattle, WA, 2001), by permission of the author.

"Late Fragment," by Raymond Carver, copyright © 1989 by The Estate of Raymond Carver, from *A New Path to the Waterfall*. Used by permission of Grove/Atlantic, Inc.

"On My Mother's Death: Harvesting" and "Reins" by Sharon Chmielarz, were previously published in *Stranger in the House* (Poetry Harbor, Duluth, MN). "On My Mother's Death: Harvesting" was first published in *Pennsylvania English*. Reprinted by permission of the author.

"Father's Diagnosis: Naming Names," by David Chura is reprinted from *Essential Love: Poems about Mothers, and Fathers, Daughters and Sons* (Grayson Books, 200) by permission of the author.

"the raising of lazarus," by Lucille Clifton, from *Good Woman: Poems and a Memoir,*

"Husband," by Mary C. McCarthy, was published in *Proposing on the Brooklyn Bridge: Poems About Marriage*, edited by Ginny Lowe Connors (Grayson Books, 2003), and reprinted by permission of the author.

"Cure," by Kathleeen McGookey, is reprinted from *Great River Review* (Volume 49, Fall/ Winter, 2008) by permission of the author.

"The Weight," by Ann McGovern, was first published by *Confrontation*. Reprinted by permission of the author.

"Potatoes," by Ethna McKiernan, is reprinted by permission of Salmon Poetry, Cliffs of Moher, Clare, Ireland, from *The One Who Swears You Can't Start Over* (2002) and by permission of the author.

"When I Am Asked," by Lisel Mueller, is reprinted from *Alive Together: New and Selected Poems* (LSU Press, 1996). Copyright © by Lisel Mueller and reprinted by permission of LSU Press.

"My Grandmother in the Stars," by Naomi Shihab Nye, is reprinted from *19 Varieties of Gazelle* (Greenwillow, 2002) by permission of the author.

"Close to Death," by Sharon Olds, from *The Father*. Copyright © 1992 by Sharon Olds, and reprinted by permission of Alfred A. Knopf a division of Random House, Inc.

"In Blackwater Woods," by Mary Oliver, from *American Primitive*. Copyright © 1978, 1979, 1980, 1981, 1982, 1983 by Mary Oliver. Reprinted by permission of Little, Brown & Company.

"When Death Comes By," by Mary Oliver, from *New and Selected Poems*, Volume 1 (Beacon Press, 2005). Copyright © 2005 by Mary Oliver. Reprinted by permission of Beacon Press.

"Migrations," by Sheila Packa, first appeared in *Ploughshares* (Spring, 1993) and also in *The Mother Tongue* (Caylx Press, Duluth, MN, 2007). Copyright © 2007 by Sheila Packa and reprinted with her permission.

"Dans Macabre," by Nancy Paddock, was published in *Trust the Wild Heart* (Red Dragonfly Press, 2006) and reprinted by permission of the author.

"The Death of a Parent," by Linda Pastan, from *A Fraction of Darkness*. Copyright © 1985 by Linda Pastan. Used by permission of Linda Pastan and W. W. Norton & Company, Inc.

"Go Gentle," by Linda Pastan, from *Carnival Evening: New and Selected Poems 1968-1998*. Copyright © 1975 by Linda Pastan, Used by permission of Linda Pastan and W. W. Norton & Company.

"How to Save the Day," by Roger Pfingston, was first published in *Triplopia* (2005) and reprinted by permission of the author.

"Making You Live This Way," by Andrea Potos, was previously published in *Yaya's Cloth* (Iris Press, 2007) and reprinted by permission of the author.

"Allowing Grace," by Judith E. Prest, was first published in *Peer Glass: An Anthology of Writing from Hudson Valley Peer Groups* (Hudson Valley Writer's Guild, Albany, New York), copyright © 2001 by Judith Prest and reprinted with her permission.

"Tattered Kaddish," by Adrienne Rich, copyright © 2002, 1991 by Adrienne Rich, from *The Fact of a Doorframe: Selected Poems 1950-2001*. Used by permission of Adrienne Rich and

About the Editors

JIM PERLMAN was born and raised in Minneapolis where his interest in poetry began in high school. In 1977, after editing various local literary magazines, he founded Holy Cow! Press. He earned a B.A. in Writing from the University of Arizona and a M.A. in English from the University of Iowa. He edited the poetry anthology *Brother Songs: A Male Anthology of Poetry* (1979) and, with Ed Folsom and Dan Campion, co-edited *Walt Whitman: The Measure of His Song* (1981, rev. ed., 1998). He and his family moved to Duluth, Minnesota in 1988, where he co-founded the Spirit Lake Poetry series, and helped establish the Duluth poet laureate project.

DEBORAH COOPER has been writing poetry for twenty years and has worked collaboratively with visual artists, musicians and dancers. Her work has been published in numerous literary journals and anthologies. She and her husband Joel, a printmaker, have exhibited their collaborative images throughout the Midwest. Deborah has used poetry extensively in her work as a hospice chaplain and teaches writing classes for those who are grieving the loss of a loved one. She also conducts workshops on the interfacing of poetry and spirituality. Deborah is the author of four small collections of poems, most recently *Between the Ceiling & the Moon*, published by Finishing Line Press as part of their New Women's Voices Series.

MARA HART has been a university librarian, has taught English and Women's Studies at the University of Minnesota, Duluth and has been a poetry editor of three literary periodicals. She teaches memoir writing, edits, and mentors writers. She believes strongly in the importance of writing one's life stories. Mara writes memoir in prose and poetry. Her work has appeared in *Sing! Heavenly Muse, Lifeboat, Poetry Claremont, Dust & Fire, Minnesota Literature,*

Erotic Justice, and *Trail Guide* among other places. In 2007 she edited *Lovecraft's New York Circle: The Kalem Club,* 1924-1927, published by Hippocampus Press, New York.

PAMELA J. MITTLEFEHLDT discovered the wonders and rigors of poetry in junior high school, when she had to memorize "The Highwayman" three consecutive years. She has taught literature and writing in high schools, community colleges, and universities. She is Professor Emerita of American Studies /Community Studies at St. Cloud State University in Minnesota. Currently, she is working on a collection of essays about the meaning of place, and is exploring the power of poetry and story to transform our lives as individuals and as communities.

ABOUT THE COVER ARTIST

JOEL COOPER has been a fine art screen printer for twenty years and has a portfolio of over 125 prints. He loves the screen process—it is slow, contemplative, and very exciting as the final vibrant colors are squeeged and come to life. His work reflects living on the shores of Lake Superior as well as his travels to Wales, Ireland, and Italy. Joel's work is exhibited throughout the Midwest in galleries and museums. Twelve of his shows have been in collaboration with wife/poet Deborah Gordon Cooper. For further information, please visit their on-line gallery: www.cooperartpoetry.com.

Subject Index

We offer this subject index as a guide to the poems herein, whose primary focus is:

Child: pages 21, 25, 66, 76, 84, 183 and 212.

Extended Family: pages 33 and 225.

Father: pages 24, 31, 44, 47, 52, 57, 58, 59, 60, 65, 74, 81, 83, 90, 95, 100, 101, 106, 109, 113, 118, 119, 125, 127, 128, 137, 144, 145, 146, 153, 156, 166, 179, 186, 191, 194, 202, 205, 207, 209, 210, 215 and 220.

Friend: pages 17, 20, 39, 55, 104, 108, 111, 116, 122, 147, 155, 181, 184 and 222.

Grandparent: pages 35, 37, 54, 61, 63, 130, 134, 142, 148, 149, 159 and 177.

Meditation on Death: pages 26, 32, 49, 50, 51, 73, 80, 89, 92, 97, 99, 112, 131, 133, 138, 140, 152, 158, 160, 162, 163, 168, 192, 193, 214, 217 and 223.

Mother: pages 19, 23, 27, 29, 34, 42, 43, 45, 46, 56, 70, 72, 77, 91, 94, 96, 102, 106, 114, 125, 127, 129, 135, 144, 145, 150, 165, 169, 173, 179, 187, 188, 189, 199, 200, 210 and 218.

Sibling: pages 170, 176, 196 and 198.

Spouse/Lover: pages 79, 87, 93, 121, 123, 126, 161, 175 and 204.

CPSIA information can be obtained
at www.ICGtesting.com
Printed in the USA
FSHW01n2303031018
52594FS

9 780977 945894